THE WELFARE INDUSTRY

Charles D. Hobbs

The Heritage Foundation

Washington, D.C.

CHARLES D. HOBBS is currently president of his own independent public policy and management consulting firm, Charles D. Hobbs, Inc., in Sacramento, California. From 1970 to 1972 he was Chief Deputy Director of Social Welfare for California and was one of the principal architects of the California Welfare Reform Program which resulted in a $700 million per year reduction in projected state and local welfare costs while providing higher benefits to people in need. From 1972 to 1973 he was a member of the California Governor's Tax Reduction Task Force and in 1974 he was a participant in the President's Economic Summit Conference on Inflation. After graduating from Northwestern University, Mr. Hobbs served in the U.S. Air Force and was later a Woodrow Wilson Fellow at the University of California in Los Angeles. He has written for a number of scholarly journals and is the co-author (with Stephen L. Powlesland) of *Retirement Security Reform: Restructuring the Social Security System* (Institute for Liberty and Community, Concord, Vermont, 1975).

Library of Congress Cataloging in Publication Data

75-52899

ISBN 0-89195-022-2

©1978 by The Heritage Foundation
513 C Street, N.E.
Washington, D.C. 20002

Table of Contents

Tables

Introduction

The purpose of this monograph is to describe the scope and development of the national welfare system, a collection of government programs designed to alleviate poverty through wealth redistribution.[1]

In the context of the welfare system, "poverty" and "wealth" are relative terms used to define conditions deemed by the government appropriate for redistribution. "Poverty" refers to financial deprivation or to situations caused or exacerbated by financial deprivation. "Wealth" is principally earned income subject to federal and state wage and sales taxes.[2]

In fact, national welfare programs are essentially earnings redistribution programs in which the earned incomes of some workers are taxed to provide unearned incomes, in cash and in kind, to other workers and non-workers.[3]

Forty-four programs have been identified and cataloged. Government expenditures for these programs in 1976 totalled $187 billion. All but 2 of the 44 are federal programs and federal expenditures constitute 80 percent of total expenditures. The combined average growth of these programs between 1971 and 1976 was 25.11 percent a year, 2.5 times the GNP growth rate and 3 times the growth of wages for the same period.[4] A preliminary analysis of the 1979 federal budget shows continued growth, with 1977 welfare expenditures estimated at more than $210 billion, and 1979 expenditures projected to be more than $250 billion.

Coincident with the extraordinary growth of welfare expenditures has been the development of a national welfare industry, now composed of 5 million public and private workers distributing payments and services to 50 million beneficiaries.[5] The federal government, with its taxing power and authority to regulate the states, has controlled this industry since its inception in the 1930s, forcing goals created for the industry on the development of the welfare system. The goals are: growth of welfare expenditures at a pace faster than national economic growth, centralization of welfare control and administration in the federal government, ever-increasing complexity of welfare programs and operations, and ever-expanding welfare industry employment.

These goals have been met to a remarkable degree: expenditures are growing at 2 to 3 times the pace of the economy; all but a handful of the 44 programs are controlled by the federal government; interactions among these programs are so complex that the industry itself cannot calculate their effects; and industry employment has expanded to the point where

7

the government is a monopsony to several welfare-related service trades, particularly those providing health care.[6]

These trends are not popular. Public dissatisfaction with welfare policies and the size and cost of the programs has made reform of the welfare "mess" a perennial political issue. Yet every attempt at national reform either has not been enacted or has resulted in even faster growth and higher costs, because the welfare industry, controlling the program design and evaluation process through the federal bureaucracy, has altered reform concepts to meet its own expansionary goals.

Recognition of the power and subtlety of this altering process comes hard to political leaders, who are used to thinking and talking about individual welfare programs instead of the entire system. President Jimmy Carter recently proposed a $34 billion "comprehensive reform of the nation's welfare system,"[7] yet his proposal covers only 5 of the 44 welfare programs and less than 20 percent of total welfare expenditures.[8] Moreover, his proposal, on examination, turns out to be little more than a rehash of the 1969–71 Nixon Family Assistance Plan which, in turn, was a warmed-over version of an earlier negative income tax proposal prepared by the industry for the Johnson Administration.[9]

Welfare costs cannot be controlled by reform of one or a few programs, even if the industry can be kept from influencing design of the reform, because of the way welfare programs overlap and interact. Adding new recipients to one program adds them to a dozen others, while removing them from one program usually does not affect their eligibility for others.[10] Moreover, what might seem to be a reasonably modest benefit from a single program becomes part of an unexpectedly generous, and costly, benefit package when the combined effects of all programs are calculated.

For example, a single-parent family with 2 children, defined by the government as poor, is theoretically eligible for 23 of the 44 national welfare programs, and selective participation in a dozen or so of them can raise the value of welfare benefits to 4 or 5 times the value of the AFDC cash payments that are usually thought of as welfare. Among the programs for which this family would be eligible are Medicaid, food stamps, free nutritional supplements for mothers and infants, free school and summer meals for school-aged children, low-rent housing, free child care, family planning and other "social" services, legal aid and job training and placement. If the parent gets a job, chances are the family will remain eligible for all of these programs, including AFDC payments. Taking away the family's AFDC payments will not affect its eligibility for the other programs and in some cases will actually increase the benefits from them.[11]

Compounding of benefits through overlapping programs is the major cause of the high welfare cost growth rate. Many welfare families are better off financially, by their participation in several programs, than are the families of workers whose taxes pay for the welfare.[12]

Forcing workers to subsidize welfare recipients at higher standards of living than their own is the ultimate absurdity of the wealth redistribution theory. The problem cannot be solved by adding welfare to the incomes of more workers, as President Carter has proposed, because as long as welfare costs grow faster than wages, the welfare burden on all workers, including those receiving welfare, will increase.[13]

The costs and inequities of the welfare system are products of the policies and programs of the federally controlled welfare industry. Welfare reform must encompass the entire system, and must start with a restructuring of the industry to remove the incentives for growth, complexity, and centralization that have operated in the past.

1

The National Welfare System

Program Definition

The national welfare system consists of all public welfare programs with nationwide applicability and impact. Neither "welfare" nor "program" is defined consistently in government sources,[14] so the following criteria were established to define each welfare program: first, that it provide a coherent set of benefits; second, that the benefits meet the definition of welfare; third, that the benefits be provided in every state; and fourth, that expenditures be clearly identifiable in the federal budget or other reliable fiscal sources.[15]

The lumping together of benefits into coherent sets was accomplished by comparing legislatively-defined program goals, target populations, types of needs to be met or benefits to be provided, and organizational assignments for benefit distribution. A set of benefits was considered "coherent" if it was intended to meet a single type of "need" in a discrete population and was administered by a single agency or by agencies legislatively mandated to work together.[16]

Each set of benefits was then evaluated as to whether it constituted, in whole or in part, an attempt to alleviate poverty through wealth redistribution. Programs and parts of programs designed to serve all people regardless of economic status were discarded as not meeting the definition of welfare. Programs designed to benefit special groups or those living in special geographical areas on the basis that all members of the group or residents of the areas should be considered inherently "economically deprived," regardless of income, were included as welfare programs.[17]

Each set of benefits was then checked for nationwide applicability. If the benefits were provided in each state, even though benefit levels and eligibility criteria might vary from state to state, the program was considered to be national in scope.

Each program was then matched against the federal budget and other fiscal sources to insure that consistent and comparable expenditure presentations could be developed. This process yielded 44 programs in 7

11

general categories. Table 1 is a summary description of the programs. Each program is described separately in the next chapter.

Expenditures

Total expenditures for the 44 welfare programs in 1976 were $186.8 billion.[18] Comparable expenditures for 1971 were $82.8 billion and for

TABLE 1

Programs of the National Welfare System

Program Title	Controlling Agency*	Type of Benefits**	First Year Enacted	1976 Recipients (in millions)	Expenditure Source***	1976 Expenditures ($ in billions)†
Food Programs						
Child Nutrition	DA	Service	1946	16.8	Shared	2.379
Elderly Feeding	DA	Service	1965	N/Av.	Federal	.011
Food Donations (Commodities)	DA	Cash	1935	0.05	Shared	.008
Food Stamps	DA	Cash	1964	18.7	Shared	5.773
Special Supplemental Food (WIC)	DA	Cash	1966	0.5	Federal	.155
Special Milk	DA	Service	1966	N/Av.	Federal	.144
Housing Programs						
Rural Housing	DA	Multiple	1949	N/Av.	Federal	.128
Lower Income Housing Assistance	HUD	Service	1974	N/Av.	Federal	.269e
Homeownership Assistance	HUD	Service	1968	N/Av.	Federal	.919e
Rent Supplements	HUD	Service	1965	N/Av.	Federal	.219e
Rental Housing	HUD	Service	1968	N/Av.	Federal	.464e
Low-Rent Public Housing	HUD	Service	1937	N/Av.	Federal	1.617e
College Housing Grants	HUD	Service	1950	N/Av.	Federal	.020e
Health Programs						
Public Health Services	HEW	Service	1946	5–8	Federal	.785
Medicaid	HEW	Service	1966	23.9	Shared	14.666
Medicare (Hospital)	HEW	Service	1965	6.1	Federal	12.574
Medicare (Supplemental Medical)	HEW	Service	1965	14.0	Federal	3.033
Community Mental Health	HEW	Service	1963	N/Av.	Shared	.752
Community Drug Abuse Treatment	HEW	Service	1966	N/Av.	Shared	.474
Community Alcoholism Treatment	HEW	Service	1970	N/Av.	Shared	.303
Cash Assistance Programs						
Social Security Old Age and Survivors Insurance (OASI)	HEW	Cash	1935	27.5	Federal	49.000e
Social Security Disability Insurance (DI)	HEW	Cash	1956	4.4	Federal	7.350e
Special Benefits for Disabled Coal Miners	HEW	Cash	1969	0.5	Federal	1.004
Supplemental Security Income (SSI)	HEW	Cash	1935	4.3	Shared	6.363
Public Assistance Grants (AFDC)	HEW	Cash	1935	11.6	Shared	10.666
Refugee Assistance	HEW	Multiple	1962	0.1	Federal	.295
General Assistance	States	Multiple	—	1.3	States	1.400e

12

TABLE 1

Programs of the National Welfare System (cont'd)

Program Title	Controlling Agency*	Type of Benefits**	First Year Enacted	1976 Recipients (in millions)	Expenditure Source***	1976 Expenditures ($ in billions)†
Employment and Work Training Programs						
Work Incentive (WIN)	HEW/ DL	Multiple	1967	0.03	Shared	.395e
Comprehensive Employment and Training Assistance (CETA)	DL	Multiple	1973	N/Av.	Federal	4.982
Employment Service	DL	Service	1933	4.2	Federal	.532
Job Corps	DL	Multiple	1964	0.06	Federal	.134
Community Service Employment for Older Americans	DL	Cash	1973	0.02	Federal	.038
Unemployment Compensation	DL	Cash	1935	3.5	Shared	20.501
Railroad Unemployment Insurance	DL	Cash	1938	0.2	Federal	.267
Workers Compensation	States	Multiple	—	N/Av.	Shared	8.000e
Education Programs						
Financial Assistance for Elementary and Secondary Education	HEW	Service	1965	5–10	Federal	2.451
Financial Assistance for Higher Education	HEW	Service	1965	1.5–2	Federal	2.590
Service and Miscellaneous Programs						
Public Assistance Services (AFDC)	HEW	Service	1935	12–15	Shared	3.702
Human Development Services	HEW	Service	1964	1.5–2	Shared	1.846
ACTION Domestic	AC-TION	Service	1964	N/Av.	Federal	.100
Legal Services	LSC	Service	1964	N/Av.	Federal	.092
Veterans Benefits	VA	Multiple	1917	7–9	Federal	18.415
Indian Benefits	DI	Multiple	1921	.45-.55	Federal	1.297
Community Services	CSA	Multiple	1964	N/Av.	Federal	.650

*DA = U.S. Department of Agriculture
HUD = U.S. Department of Housing and Urban Development
HEW = U.S. Department of Health, Education, and Welfare
DL = U.S. Department of Labor
ACTION = Federal ACTION Agency
LSC = Federal Legal Services Corporation
VA = Federal Veterans Administration
DI = U.S. Department of Interior
CSA = Federal Community Services Administration

**See text for definitions of cash and service benefits. Multiple benefits include both cash and service.

***"Shared" programs are those funded jointly by federal and state governments.

†"e" = estimated. See individual program descriptions in following chapter for explanations of estimates.

13

1975 were $159.4 billion. Expenditures in 1971 represented 7.8 percent of the GNP; 1975 expenditures, 10.6 percent; and 1976 expenditures, 11.0 percent.[19]

Twenty-one of the programs, including at least 2 in 6 of the 7 general categories, had expenditures in 1976 in excess of $1 billion and total expenditures for these 21 "billion-dollar-plus" programs were $178.8 billion, or 95.7 percent of total welfare expenditures.

Five programs had expenditures in 1976 in the range of $500 million to $1 billion, 12 had expenditures in the range of $100 million to $500 million, and the remaining 6 had expenditures of less than $100 million.

The 10 most expensive programs in 1976 are listed in Table 2.

TABLE 2

The 10 Highest Expenditure Welfare Programs in 1976

	($ in billions)
1. Social Security (OASI)	49.0[20]
2. Unemployment Compensation	20.5
3. Veterans Benefits	18.4
4. Medicaid	14.7
5. Medicare (Hospital)	12.6
6. Public Assistance Grants (AFDC)	10.7
7. Workers Compensation	8.0
8. Social Security (DI)	7.4[21]
9. Supplemental Security Income (SSI)	6.4
10. Food Stamps	5.8

Total expenditures for these 10 programs were 153.5 billion, or 82.2 percent of total welfare expenditures.

Expenditure Sources

Twenty-nine of the 44 programs are financed completely from federal funds, one (General Assistance) is financed completely from state and local funds, and 14 are "shared" programs, jointly funded by federal and state (and sometimes local) governments.

Shared programs are of two types: the first, exemplified by Public Assistance Grants (AFDC), provides either a federal match for state expenditures or a fixed federal percentage of total expenditures; the second, exemplified by Unemployment Compensation, includes a federal expenditure component not tied to the amount of either state or total expenditures.

Shared programs of the first type are "carrot and stick" programs: they combine proportionate federal funding with federal regulation of program benefit levels to force constant increases in state and local expenditures.[22] Twelve of the 14 shared programs are of this type. Of the 21

14

"billion-dollar-plus" programs, 9 are also shared programs—7 of the first type. Of the 10 most expensive programs, 6 are also shared programs—4 of the first type.

Federal funding comes either from general revenues or special payroll taxes, such as social security taxes, levied to support specific programs. Of the 29 programs financed completely from federal sources, 24 are funded only from general revenues; 2 (Medicare—Hospital— and Special Benefits for Coal Miners) are funded from a mixture of general and special revenues; and 3 (Social Security—OASI and DI— and Railroad Unemployment Insurance) are funded only from special revenues.

In the 14 "sharing" programs, federal portions are all taken from general revenues in 12, and from a mixture of general and special revenues in 2 (Unemployment Compensation and Workers Compensation).

Expenditure Growth

Between 1971 and 1976 the growth of the 44 welfare programs combined was 125.54 percent, an average annual rate of 25.11 percent. By comparison, in the same period the federal budget grew at an average annual rate of 15.34 percent, the GNP at 10.26 percent, the cost of living at 8.66 percent, and average gross/hourly wages in private industry at 7.67 percent.[23] The 1979 federal budget shows continued growth at a slightly slower pace: 1977 welfare expenditures are estimated to have totalled more than $210 billion, and 1979 expenditures are projected, very conservatively, at $250 billion.

As a percentage of the GNP, welfare expenditures between 1971 and 1976 grew from 7.78 percent to 11.62 percent. As a percentage of the federal budget, federal outlays for welfare grew in the same period from 31.69 percent to 40.95 percent.

The growth rates of individual programs varied from one that actually declined (Food Donations) to one that experienced a sixteen-fold annual increase (Rural Housing Program). Seven programs grew at average rates above 100 percent a year, 5 at 50 to 100 percent, 8 at 30 to 50 percent, and 9 at 20 to 30 percent. Only 9 of the 44 programs grew more slowly than the federal budget and only 6 more slowly than the GNP.

As a group, the "billion-dollar-plus" programs grew slightly faster than all of the programs combined: 28.06 percent compared to 25.18 percent. Only one of the 21 "billion-dollar-plus" programs (Financial Assistance for Elementary and Secondary Education) grew more slowly than the GNP.

Four major federal departments—Agriculture; Health, Education, and Welfare; Housing and Urban Development; and Labor—each manage several welfare programs. The breakdown of each department's share of welfare expenditures and welfare growth is as follows:

15

TABLE 3

Multiple Program Management by Federal Departments

	Agriculture	HEW	HUD	Labor
Number of Programs[24]	7	18	6	8
1971 Welfare Expenditures (in billions of $)	2.7	57.0	1.0	10.6
% of Total 1971 Welfare Expenditures[25]	3.3%	68.8%	1.2%	12.8%
1976 Welfare Expenditures (in billions of $)	8.6	118.2	3.5	34.8
% of Total 1976 Welfare Expenditures[26]	4.6%	63.3%	1.9%	18.6%
Average Annual Growth Rate	43.7%	21.5%	51.6%	45.7%

Welfare Recipients

Due to inadequate recipient population data for many programs and to the fact that many, probably most, welfare recipients receive benefits from several programs concurrently, the total number of persons receiving welfare benefits cannot be determined precisely.[27] In 17 of the programs cataloged, recipient data were too scanty or inconsistent for reliable presentation and in 6 others, available data allowed only gross estimates of numbers of recipients.

A 1973 Congressional report estimated that the 119 million "beneficiaries" of income transfer programs in 1972 "were actually comprised of no more than 60 million different individuals."[28] This figure, supposedly based on known overlaps among cash payments and public housing programs, is too high, probably by 25 to 30 percent.[29]

A more accurate estimate can be made by examining health care benefit programs, for which fairly accurate recipient population figures are available, and among which significant variances in benefit levels and costs to the recipients for similar services make overlap estimates more reliable. Medicaid, Medicare (Supplemental Medical), and the medical component of Veterans Benefits make up a group of health programs which can be used for such an estimate.

Added to this probable total should be a few million persons who are not eligible for any of these health benefits, but are receiving some other form of welfare.[31] Thus, estimates of 39 million individual welfare recipients in 1971, 50 million in 1976, and an average annual growth rate of 5.8 percent appear reasonable.

16

TABLE 4

Estimate of Total Number of Welfare Recipients
Based on Health Programs

	Recipients in Millions	
	1971	1976
Medicaid	18.2	23.9
Medicare (Supplemental Medical)	19.8	24.0
Veterans Benefits (Medical)	3.8	6.1
Apparent Total	41.8	54.0
Probable Overlap[30]	-5.0	-6.5
Probable Total Individuals	36.8	47.5

Benefits

The wide variety of benefits available in the different welfare programs may be summarized as: cash, where the benefits are provided directly to the recipient as cash or some other negotiable item such as food stamps; and service, where the benefits are provided through the services of the government or a third party reimbursed by the government.

Twenty-one of the 44 programs provide cash benefits, and 11 of these provide only cash or other negotiables. Of the 11, 6 are "billion-dollar-plus" programs which are also among the 10 most expensive programs (Social Security—OASI and DI, Supplemental Security Income—SSI, Public Assistance Grants—AFDC, Unemployment Compensation, and Food Stamps).

Thirty-three programs provide service benefits and 23 of these provide only services. Of the 23, only 2 are among the 10 most expensive programs (Medicaid and Medicare—Hospital) and 9 are "billion-dollar-plus" programs.

Of the 10 programs which combine cash and services, 2 are among the 10 most expensive programs (Veterans Benefits and Workers Compensation) and 5 are "billion-dollar-plus" programs.

There is an interesting correlation between types of benefits and ages of the programs. Of the 11 cash-only programs, 7 were enacted prior to 1960;[32] whereas 17 of the 23 service-only programs have been enacted since 1960. More than half, 12 of 21, of the programs providing cash benefits were enacted before 1960, compared with one-third, 11 of 33, of programs providing service benefits.

Program Control and Administration

Only 2 nationwide welfare programs (General Assistance and Workers Compensation) are controlled by the states; the remaining 42 are con-

17

trolled, wholly or chiefly, by laws and agencies of the federal government. The degree of federal control varies from program to program, depending on how authority is delegated in the enabling legislation and how much of the program cost is borne by the federal government.

The 29 programs totally funded by the federal government are also controlled totally by the federal government, either through direct federal administration, in 20 of the 29, or through federal regulations which leave little or no administrative discretion to state and local agencies which carry out the programs. Four of the 10 most expensive programs and 11 of the 21 "billion-dollar-plus" programs are funded completely by the federal government.

Thus, while state and local governments administer 24 programs, 17 alone and 7 in conjunction with the federal government, they exercise no administrative control over 9 programs that are federally funded, limited administrative control over 13 of the remaining 15 that are established by federal law, and total administrative control over only the 2 that are not the products of federal law.

Program Age

Two decades—the '30s and the '60s—produced the bulk of the nation's welfare programs. Ten programs were enacted in the 1930s and 20 more were enacted in the 1960s. Only 4 were enacted before 1930,[33] 5 between 1940 and 1960, and 5 since 1970.

In recent years, however, the legislation of welfare policies and programs has been accomplished principally through amendments to existing acts. Twenty-six of the 44 programs, including all of the 10 most expensive, have been significantly expanded in the last 10 years through amendments.[34]

There is a strong correlation between the age of a program and the size of its expenditures. Thirteen of the 21 "billion-dollar-plus" programs and 8 of the 10 most expensive programs were enacted before 1960. All 4 of the programs originally enacted between 1930, and 7 of the 10 programs enacted in the '30s are now "billion-dollar-plus" programs, whereas only 7 of the 20 enacted in the '60s are in that category.

Program Overlap

There are two senses in which welfare programs may be said to overlap. The first and more general condition occurs when one person is eligible for two or more welfare programs. This kind of overlap is almost universal among the 44 programs, since only 5 of them restrict eligibility on the basis of participation in other programs, and even these preclude overlapping eligibility for only one or a few other programs. In fact, many programs,

18

and especially the basic cash assistance programs (Public Assistance—AFDC, Supplemental Security Income—SSI, Social Security—OASI and DI, and Unemployment Compensation), encourage applicants to compound their benefits by applying for overlapping programs.

The second and more limited overlap condition occurs when a person is eligible for benefits from two or more programs that meet precisely the same "needs," such as for food or housing or health care. Only 21 programs, or fewer than half, have even this limited kind of overlap restriction.

There are two absolute restrictions related to eligibility overlap among the cash assistance programs. The first is that a father-headed family is not eligible for AFDC cash payments if the father is eligible for unemployment compensation. This exclusion does not apply to a mother-headed family. The second is that no person can be simultaneously eligible for AFDC and SSI. This restriction has little effect on actual overlapping of benefits, since AFDC is awarded not to individuals but to families, and a family may receive AFDC even if SSI recipients are living with the family.

The only absolute restriction related to eligibility overlap among food programs is that no one may simultaneously receive food stamps and food commodities (Food Donations Program). Since the Food Stamp Program was designed to replace commodities, the effect of this restriction has been to gradually reduce expenditures for food commodities, but the reduction has only fractionally offset the extraordinary rise in food stamp expenditures. Also, the intent of eliminating overlap between these programs has been partially thwarted by the siphoning off of food commodities to other programs, such as Child Nutrition and Elderly Feeding, which provide benefits to institutions instead of persons. Thus, an elderly food stamp recipient may take some of his meals at a senior citizen's center which receives food commodities from the Elderly Feeding Program.

Eligibility overlap restrictions among housing programs are predicated on the assumption that one person can inhabit only one residence at a time. A recipient of an urban housing benefit should not, therefore, receive simultaneously a rural housing benefit, at least theoretically. The Rural Housing Program is operated by the Department of Agriculture and urban housing programs are operated by local agencies under the control of HUD and there appears to be little coordination between the two. Within the HUD programs the same assumption of single residence applies, so that one person cannot simultaneously live in low-rent public housing and receive homeownership assistance or a rent supplement for a privately-owned residence.

Within the health programs there is probably little or no overlap between either of the Medicare programs and Medicaid, not because of restrictions, but because anyone eligible for the completely paid Medicaid benefits would be foolish to pay the partial costs and premiums that Medicare requires. There is probably no overlap among job training and employment programs, since participation in one is all that is necessary to insure eligibility for cash assistance programs.

With these relatively minor exceptions, program overlap and the compounding of benefits it can produce are theoretically unlimited.[35] In 1969 the Congressional Research Service demonstrated that a welfare family in Portland, Oregon, consisting of a mother and four children could theoretically compound $2,808 in AFDC cash payments with benefits of 14 other programs to a total untaxed income of $13,799, equal to a before-tax worker's income of $16,500.[36] Given the growth of welfare benefits since 1969, 1978 benefits to the same family would be 50 percent to 75 percent higher. Looked at another way, a low-income family consisting of a mother and two children, one an infant and the other in school, is theoretically eligible for 23 of the 44 national welfare programs. Adding a father to the family raises the number of programs to 26. Then, adding a teen-aged child and a grandfather, the family becomes theoretically eligible for 35 of the 44 programs.[37]

Beyond a certain point such theoretical calculations only serve to point up the absurd complexities of the welfare system. Here, for example is a family of eight which could theoretically qualify for 39 programs. It consists of an alcoholic Indian veteran in job training and going to college who lives in New York City with his 75 year-old retired father, his 60 year-old work-disabled mother, his disabled coal miner brother now on sick leave from a railroad job, his recently unemployed sister-in-law, and his mentally retarded Cuban refugee wife and their three children, one an infant hemophiliac, one a ten year-old junkie, and one a teen-aged school dropout. If such a family exists, it could become wealthy on welfare.

It is not absurd, however, to envision two-generation families benefitting simultaneously from 15 or more programs and three-generation families benefitting from 20 or more programs.[38]

Given the growth rates of total welfare expenditures as compared with the relatively much smaller increases in welfare population, this degree of overlap must, in fact be more the rule than the exception.

Summary

In summary, the programs making up the national welfare system are characterized by extremely high expenditure growth rates and extensive overlapping of benefits and beneficiaries. The older the program, the more likely it is to be one of the most expensive, and the younger the program, the more likely it is to provide service instead of cash. Control of the programs, and thus of the welfare system, is almost totally in the hands of the federal government, and within the federal government control is concentrated in HEW, Labor, HUD, and Agriculture. The welfare system can therefore be characterized as expansionary, complex, centralized, and heading toward the provision of services instead of cash.

2

Welfare Programs

This chapter contains brief individual descriptions of the 44 programs which make up the national welfare system. Basic data sources, unless otherwise noted, are: *The Budget of the United States Government, Appendix, 1973, 1977, 1978; The United States Statistical Abstract;* and *The Federal Catalog of Domestic Assistance Programs, 1973, 1976, 1977.*

Food Programs
Program: CHILD NUTRITION PROGRAM

Components: School Lunch Program, School Breakfast Program, Summer Food Program, Child Care Program.

Benefits: Subsidized breakfasts and lunches for children in school or child care facilities. Reduced-price and free breakfasts and lunches for children from low-income families in school or child care facilities. Free summer meals for school-aged children in designated "areas of economic need."

Control: Federal government: Department of Agriculture (Food and Nutrition Service).

Administration: State governments through public and private schools and child care facilities.

Recipients:	1971	1975	1976
Children Receiving:			
Subsidized Meals	17,500,000	16,125,000	15,582,000
Reduced-Price Meals		626,000	993,000
	6,200,000		
Free Meals		13,254,000	15,866,000

Eligibility: All children in those schools or child care facilities which operate a federally approved meal program are eligible for subsidized breakfasts and lunches. Children from families with incomes between the poverty level and 195% of the poverty level are eligible for reduced-price break-

23

fasts and lunches. Children from families below the poverty level are eligible for free breakfasts and lunches. All children in "areas of economic need" are eligible for free summer meals, regardless of family income.

Cost:	1971	1975	1976
Subsidized Meals:			
Federal	$227,150,000	$489,978,000	$577,164,000
State	$13,629,000	$39,198,000	$46,173,000
Reduced-Price Meals (All Federal)	> $389,750,000	$60,367,000	$104,077,000
Free Meals (All Federal)		$1,281,439,000	$1,651,877,000
TOTAL	$630,529,000	$1,870,982,000	$2,379,291,000

Annual Growth: Average 1971–1976: total program = 55.47%; reduced price and free meals = 70.06%.

Financing: For subsidized meals, the federal government pays 25% of cost or as much more as the percentage by which a given state's average per-capita income falls below the national average; states pay, from general revenues, a growing percentage of the remainder (1973 = 6%, 1975 and 1976 = 8%, 1977 and thereafter = 10%). For reduced-price and free meals, the federal government pays the total cost.

Overlap: All other programs. Participation in this program does not affect eligibility for or benefit levels in any other program, including other food programs.

History: Enacted in 1946 as a general subsidy for school lunches, this program has been increasingly "welfarized" through a series of amendments, especially those in 1966, 1968, and 1970, which expanded the program to breakfasts and child care institutions, and established federal payment for reduced-price and free meals for children of low-income families.

Program: ELDERLY FEEDING PROGRAM

Benefits: Food commodities for institutional preparation of meals for elderly low-income persons.

Control: Federal government: Department of Agriculture (Food and Nutrition Service).

Administration: State and local governments through public and private centers for the elderly.

Recipients:	1971	1975	1976
Meals Served	N/Appl.	54,100,000	97,500,000

24

Eligibility: All elderly persons who go to authorized senior citizens' meal centers.

Cost:	1971	1975	1976
TOTAL (All Federal)	N/Appl.	$5,413,000	$11,300,000

Annual Growth: 1975–1976 = 108.76%.

Financing: Federal subsidy amounted to 15¢ per meal in 1975 and 16.5¢ per meal in 1976.

Overlap: All other programs affecting the aged. Participation in this program does not affect eligibility for or benefit levels in any other program.

History: An outgrowth of the Older Americans Act of 1965, this program appears ready to blossom into another high-growth welfare program. Budgeted costs for 1978 are $30,000,000.

Program: FOOD DONATIONS PROGRAM (Commodities)

Benefits: Provides government-purchased basic foods to low-income households and individuals, and to institutions serving the poor.

Control: Federal government: Department of Agriculture (Food and Nutrition Service).

Administration: State and local governments.

Recipients:	1971	1975	1976
Persons Receiving Commodities	3,600,000	330,000	50,000

Eligibility: Certification of individual, household, or institutional need by local welfare authorities, coupled with unavailability of food stamps.

Cost:	1971	1975	1976
Federal	$347,000,000	$35,290,000	$7,937,000
State		Not Available	

Financing: The federal government pays the entire cost of the food. State and local governments pay administrative, storage, and transportation costs. Institutions receiving commodities may be assessed costs of the state distribution system.

Overlap: All other programs except Food Stamps.

History: Enacted in the '30s as a combined agricultural subsidy and welfare program, this program is being phased out in favor of food stamps. It remains available only to those who cannot yet utilize food stamps.

Program: FOOD STAMP PROGRAM

Benefits: Provides, to low-income households and individuals, free stamps which may be redeemed for food at regular retail stores.

Control: Federal government: Department of Agriculture (Food and Nutrition Service).

Administration: State and local governments.

Recipients:	*1971*	*1975*	*1976*
Persons Receiving Food Stamps (Average During Year)	9,368,000	17,100,000	18,700,000

Eligibility: Low-income "households" of one or more individuals. The value of the food stamps issued to a household is based upon household size and income. The average value per-person per-month for 1976 was $23.77.

Cost:	*1971*	*1975*	*1976*
Federal	$1,574,238,000	$4,691,837,000	$5,596,787,000
State	$17,800,000	$91,312,000	$176,102,000
TOTAL	*$1,592,038,000*	*$4,883,149,000*	*$5,772,889,000*

Annual Growth: Average 1971–1976 = 52.52%.

Financing: The federal government pays the entire value of the food stamps plus 50% of state administrative costs. State and local governments pay the remaining 50% of administrative costs.

Overlap: All other programs except Food Donations. Although welfare grant programs, such as AFDC and SSI, include payments deemed by the government to be adequate for food, benefits of these programs are not reduced by participation in the Food Stamp Program.

History: Enacted in 1964 as a part-subsidy, part-welfare program in which low-income families could purchase food stamps at less than redemption value, the program has been amended several times to expand eligibility and reduce the cost of stamps to recipients. In 1977 the purchase requirement was dropped altogether, reducing the recipient participation cost to zero. The easy negotiability of the stamps and restriction of their use to food products has fostered an extensive black market.

Program: SPECIAL SUPPLEMENTAL FOOD PROGRAM FOR WOMEN, INFANTS, AND CHILDREN (WIC)

Benefits: Provides iron-fortified infant formula and breakfast cereal, milk, cheese, and high-vitamin fruit juices as supplements to regular diet for undernourished or low-income mothers and children.

Control: Federal government: Department of Agriculture (Food and Nutrition Service).

Administration: Local public and private health care agencies serving low-income areas.

Recipients:	1971	1975	1976
Persons Receiving Benefits	N/Appl.	132,000	520,094

Eligibility: Pregnant or lactating women and infants and children who live in an area designated as an "area of need" and are eligible for medical care at less than full charge.

Cost:	1971	1975	1976
TOTAL (All Federal)	N/Appl.	$98,941,000	$155,003,000

Annual Growth: 1975–1976 = 56.67%. Budgeted for 1978 to serve 910,000 persons at a cost of $335,742,000.

Financing. All federal, although states must bear administrative costs in excess of 10% of the total federal grant.

Overlap: All other programs. Participation in this program does not affect eligibility for or benefit levels in any other program.

History: The present program is a major 1974 expansion of a program originally enacted in 1966. It is one of the fastest-growing of all welfare programs, principally because it is intended as a supplement to other programs, and is promoted by health care facilities as well as welfare agencies.

Program: SPECIAL MILK PROGRAM FOR CHILDREN

Benefits: Reduced-price or free milk for children attending participating schools and other child care facilities.

Control: Federal government: Department of Agriculture (Food and Nutrition Service).

Administration: State education agencies or, if such agencies are prohibited from disbursing federal funds to private institutions, Food and Nutrition Service regional offices.

Recipients:	1971	1975	1976
Half-Pints of Milk Served	2,570,000,000	2,133,000,000	N/Avbl.

Eligibility: All children who attend any participating school or child care facility are eligible for reduced-price milk. In facilities designated as "needy" by state and federal authorities, milk is free to all students.

Cost:	1971	1975	1976
TOTAL (All Federal)	$93,297,000	$124,938,000	$143,950,000

Annual Growth: Average 1971–1976 = 10.86%.

Financing: The federal government subsidizes each half-pint of reduced-price milk served. The subsidy in 1971 was 3.55¢; in 1975, 5.8¢; in 1976,

6.2¢. States pay the remainder by charging the recipients. The federal government pays the entire cost of free milk to "needy" schools.

Overlap: All other programs, except that the first half-pint served with any meal which is reimbursed under the Child Nutrition Program is excluded from federal payment by this program.

History: Enacted in 1966, this program is redundant with several others, and the Executive Branch has twice tried, unsuccessfully, to phase it out. The cost of the program continues to rise, despite the overlaps and a decline in the amount of milk served, because of inflation and the federal policy of certifying more and more schools as "needy."

Housing Programs
Program: RURAL HOUSING PROGRAM

Components: Farm Labor Housing Loans and Grants, Low to Moderate Housing Loans, Rural Housing Site Loans, Rural Rental Housing Loans, Very-Low Income Housing Repair Loans, Rural Self-Help Housing Technical Assistance.

Benefits: Grants, direct loans, and federal guarantees and insurance of loans to low-income rural families and individuals for housing assistance, and to agencies which build and manage such housing.

Control and Administration: Federal government: Department of Agriculture (Farmers Home Administration).

Recipients: Available data are too inconsistent and incomplete for reliable presentation.

Eligibility: Rural families and individuals with incomes too low to qualify for loans from usual lending sources. "Rural" is defined as being areas and communities of less than 20,000 population and not within a standard metropolitan statistical area.

Cost:	1971	1975	1976
Grants	$883,000	$6,182,000	$6,084,000
Loans	$683,000	$125,603,000	$122,000,000
TOTAL (All Federal)	$1,566,000	$131,785,000	$128,084,000

Annual Growth: Average 1971–1976 = 1,615.8%.

Financing: All federal. Farm labor housing grants require 10% from "other sources," but this requirement can be met by a federal loan.

Overlap: All other programs except urban housing programs.

History: Most of the components of this program were enacted in the Housing Act of 1949. Administrative policy changes, especially in the past 10 years, have produced rapid growth, roughly equivalent to the growth of

28

urban housing programs, but less advertised. The program also has the same problems of lack of accomplishment and default of loans. Total government equity in the program decreased from $701,435,000 in 1971 to –$1,085,912,000 in 1978 (est), a loss of almost $1.8 billion in seven years.

Program: LOWER INCOME HOUSING ASSISTANCE PROGRAM (Section 8)

Benefits: Federal subsidies for rent, including utilities, of low-income families and individuals, through direct payments to landlords of the fair market rent in excess of 15% to 25% of family income.

Control and Administration: Federal government: Department of Housing and Urban Development (Federal Housing Administration) through contracts with local housing authorities and private owners of low-income housing projects.

Recipients:	*1971*	*1975*	*1976*
Subsidized Housing Units	N/Appl.	N/Appl.	87,000 (est)*

Eligibility: Families with annual incomes not in excess of 80% of the median family income for their metropolitan area, and who rent from local housing authorities or private owners who have agreed to lease to persons eligible for public housing. Also low-income aged, blind, and disabled individuals.

Cost:	*1971*	*1975*	*1976*
TOTAL (All Federal)	N/Appl.	N/Appl.	*$269,000,000* (est)*

Annual Growth: 1977 costs are approximately $800,000,000.

Financing: All federal.

Overlap: All other programs except Rural Housing and Homeownership Assistance.

History: A new program, enacted in 1974 and not funded until 1976, intended to expand availability of low-rent housing as well as to bolster supposedly inadequate subsidies in the Rent Supplement and Rental Housing Assistance programs. A three-fold growth in costs in the first year presages another major welfare program.

*The HUD section of the federal budget is not adequate for definition of program costs. Estimates here are those of HUD at its 1978 budget presentation to Congress.

Program: HOMEOWNERSHIP ASSISTANCE PROGRAM (Section 235)

Benefits: Federal subsidies to reduce mortgage interest and thereby enable low-income individuals and families to purchase new homes. In the origi-

29

nal version of the program, the subsidies reduced recipient mortgage interest rates to as low as 1%. The revised (1975) program lowers the recipient interest rate to 5%.

Control and Administration: Federal government: Department of Housing and Urban Development (Federal Housing Administration).

Recipients:	*1971*	*1975*	*1976*
Units Subsidized			
(End of Year)	204,832	408,915	406,000
			(est)*

Eligibility: Based on income and geared to local income limits for admission to low-rent or below-market-interest-rate housing. At least 80% of available funds must be used for families, handicapped persons, or aged persons whose annual incomes, after $300 per person deductions, are less than 135% of the upper limit for admission to low-income public housing.

Cost:	*1971*	*1975*	*1976*
Subsidy			
Payments	$121,602,000	$195,157,000	$191,000,000
			(est)*
Defaulted Mort-			
gage Payments	$167,446,000	$842,361,000	$728,281,000
			(est)*
TOTAL (All			
Federal)	*$289,048,000*	*$1,037,518,000*	*$919,281,000*
			(est)*

Annual Growth: Average 1971–1975 = 64.70%.

Financing: The federal government pays the entire interest-reduction subsidy. The recipient is expected to pay 20% of net income to make up the remainder of the mortgage payment. Mortgage defaults are made good by the federal government.

Overlap: All other programs except rent subsidy programs. Although welfare grant programs, such as AFDC and SSI, contain an adequate housing component, participation in this program does not reduce grant payments.

History: Enacted in 1968, the original program produced a high default rate and instant suburban slums. The Executive Branch tried to end the program, but a 1975 court decision forced them to continue it, but with higher recipient interest payment requirements. The revised program thus makes eligible only the most affluent of the "poor," namely those who can afford to pay a 5% mortgage interest rate on a new home.

*The HUD section of the federal budget is not adequate for definition of program costs. Estimates here are those of HUD at its 1978 budget presentation to Congress.

Program: RENT SUPPLEMENT PROGRAM

Benefits: Rent subsidies of up to 70% of fair market rental value for low-income families and individuals living in government-approved private housing projects.

Control and Administration: Federal government: Department of Housing and Urban Development (Federal Housing Administration).

Recipients:	1971	1975	1976
Units Subsidized			
(End of Year)	57,786	165,826	183,000 (est)*

Eligibility: Families and aged and handicapped individuals whose incomes are low enough to qualify them for low-rent public housing.

Cost:	1971	1975	1976
TOTAL (All			
Federal)	$44,616,000	$177,396,000	$219,000,000 (est)*

Annual Growth: Average 1971–1975 = 74.40%.

Financing: The federal government pays the entire cost of the rent subsidies. To make up the remainder of the rent, recipients are expected to pay no more than 25% of their annual income, net deductions of $300 per person.

Overlap: All other programs except Rural Housing, Low-Rent Public Housing, and Homeownership Assistance.

History: Enacted in 1965, this program is now being supplemented, despite its fantastic record of growth, by the Lower Income Housing Assistance Program for additional units not previously under contract.

*The HUD section of the federal budget is not adequate for definition of program costs. Estimates here are those of HUD at its 1978 budget presentation to Congress.

Program: RENTAL HOUSING ASSISTANCE PROGRAM (Section 236)

Benefits: Federal interest-reduction subsidy to mortagees of low-income rental property. Reduces effective mortgage interest rates to as low as 1%, enabling owners to lower rents to low-income families and individuals.

Control and Administration: Federal government: Department of Housing and Urban Development (Federal Housing Administration).

Recipients:	1971	1975	1976
Units Subsidized			
(End of Year)	32,322	400,360	459,000 (est)*

Eligibility: Subsidies are paid on the basis of how many qualified low-income renters occupy mortgagee's housing units. "Low-income" qualifications vary from community to community, but generally are the same as qualification for occupancy of low-rent public housing. Low-income renters are required to pay up to 25% of income, net deductions of $300 per person, in rent, but not more than fair market rent value.

Cost:	1971	1975	1976
TOTAL (All Federal)	$15,174,000	$384,925,000	$464,000,000 (est)*

Annual Growth: Average 1971–1975 = 609.19%. Extremely high rate due in part to fact that program was just beginning in 1971. Based on 1977 budget of $603,000,000, current growth rate is about 30% per year.

Financing: The federal government pays the entire interest-reduction subsidy to mortgage holders on behalf of mortgagees.

Overlap: All other programs except Rural Housing, Low-Rent Public Housing, and Homeownership Assistance.

History: Enacted in 1968, this program, despite its extraordinary growth rate, is now being supplemented by the Lower Income Housing Assistance Program.

*The HUD section of the federal budget is not adequate for definition of program costs. Estimates here are those of HUD at its 1978 budget presentation to Congress.

Program: LOW-RENT PUBLIC HOUSING

Benefits: Federal financing of local housing authorities to construct and operate low-income housing projects.

Control and Administration: Federal government: Department of Housing and Urban Development (Federal Housing Administration).

Recipients:	1971	1975	1976
Units in Projects (End of Year)	952,000	1,151,000	1,197,000 (est)*

Eligibility: Local housing authorities created to provide public housing to low-income families and individuals are eligible. Income limits on tenants vary from community to community, but generally require that income be at least 20% below that needed to qualify for private, non-subsidized housing.

Cost:	1971	1975	1976
TOTAL (All Federal)	$626,354,000	$1,422,034,000	$1,617,000,000 (est)*

Annual Growth: Average 1971–1975 = 31.76%.

Financing: All federal, through grants and loans to local housing authorities. There is an indirect local contribution because housing authorities make payments in lieu of property taxes which are lower than full property taxes would be.

Overlap: All other programs, except other housing programs limited to private housing, and Rural Housing.

History: Enacted in 1937, this program financed the housing components of urban renewal and its successors. Frequently expanded by amendments, particularly those of 1959 and 1970, this old program is now growing faster than it did in its urban renewal hey-day.

*The HUD section of the federal budget is not adequate for definition of program costs. Estimates here are those of HUD at its 1978 budget presentation to Congress.

Program: COLLEGE HOUSING GRANTS

Benefits: Federal debt service grants are provided to colleges and teaching hospitals to reduce the interest on loans for student housing and related facilities, ostensibly to allow colleges to house more low-income students.

Control and Administration: Federal government: Department of Housing and Urban Development (Federal Housing Administration).

Recipients:	*1971*	*1975*	*1976*
Number of Grantee Colleges and Hospitals	10	430	430

Eligibility: Colleges and teaching hospitals which are borrowing from normal lending institutions to acquire or build student housing and facilities, such as student centers, dining halls, and infirmaries.

Cost:	*1971*	*1975*	*1976*
TOTAL (All Federal Grants)	$430,000	$17,414,000	$20,000,000 (est)*

Annual Growth: Average 1971–1975 = 987.44%. Extraordinarily high growth rate due, in part, to the fact that the program was just beginning in 1971.

Financing: All federal.

Overlap: Financial Assistance for Higher Education.

History: A college welfare program. Enacted in 1950 as a low-interest direct loan program for institutions unable to borrow from normal sources, the program bloomed after 1968 when amended to provide debt service grants to institutions capable of normal borrowing. The rush for federal

33

grants forced discontinuance of the program in 1973, but not before 430 institutions had secured continuing grants based on long-term mortgage and construction loans.

*The HUD section of the federal budget is not adequate for definition of program costs. Estimates here are those of HUD at its 1978 budget presentation to Congress.

Health Programs

Program: PUBLIC HEALTH SERVICES

Components: Community Health Centers, Maternal and Child Health Services, Family Planning Services, Migrant Health Program, Health Maintenance Organizations, National Health Service Corps, Hypertension Program, Hemophilia Program, and Home Health Services.

Benefits: Free or low-cost health care through public health facilities for low-income individuals and families.

Control: Federal government: Department of Health, Education, and Welfare (Public Health Service).

Administration: Combination of federal (Public Health Service hospitals) and state (state and local public health facilities).

Recipients: During the '70s, 5,000,000 to 8,000,000 persons have received public health care annually.

Eligibility: Need for health care and willingness to accept it at public health facilities. Facilities give preference in most program components to low-income persons.

Cost:	*1971*	*1975*	*1976*
TOTAL (All Federal)	$607,434,000	$938,719,000	$785,074,000

Annual growth: Average 1971–1976 = 5.85%.

Financing: All federal, but in most states patients must pay part of cost, if able.

Overlap: All other programs.

History: This collection of services stems from the Public Health Service Act of 1946, frequently amended to expand areas of service and population served. Public health facilities have always been unpopular among low-income persons. The availability of private alternatives under Medicaid and Medicare have caused a slow decline in public health patient treatment and a relative stabilization of the public health budget in relation to other welfare programs.

Program: MEDICAID

Benefits: Government payment of virtually all medical and health-related costs for eligible low-income persons and families.

34

Control: Federal government: Department of Health, Education, and Welfare (Health Care Financing Administration).

Administration: State governments and, at state option, local governments.

Recipients:	1971	1975	1976
Persons Served	18,223,000	22,467,000	23,894,000

Eligibility: In all states, all persons receiving AFDC cash grants. In 36 states, all persons receiving SSI payments; in the remaining 14 states, SSI recipients who meet special Medicaid income requirements. In 29 states, all other persons who are "medically needy": that is, whose incomes, after allowable deductions, fall below 133% of the welfare need standard for that state.

Cost:	1971	1975	1976
Federal	$3,373,866,000	$7,059,672,000	$8,324,053,000
State and Local	$2,802,007,000	$5,577,569,000	$6,341,769,000
TOTAL	*$6,175,873,000*	*$12,637,241,000*	*$14,665,822,000*

Annual Growth: Average 1971–1976 = 27.49%.

Financing: Federal: 50% to 83% of benefit costs, depending on state per-capita income; 75% of medical administrative costs; 50% of other administrative costs. State and local governments pay the remainder.

Overlap: All other programs except, for practical purposes, Medicare, which would not be worth using if one were eligible for Medicaid.

History: Enacted in 1966, Medicaid has grown far beyond congressional expectations in number of recipients and, even more so, in cost. In addition to increasing the general tax burden, Medicaid spending policies have contributed significantly to the rapid growth of health care industry costs.

Program: MEDICARE (Social Security Hospital Insurance)

Benefits: Subsidized hospital and hospital-related medical care for the aged and disabled and their dependents and survivors.

Control and Administration: Federal government: Department of Health, Education, and Welfare (Health Care Financing Agency).

Recipients:	1971	1975	1976
Persons Enrolled:			
Aged	20,300,000	21,500,000	22,200,000
Disabled		2,100,000	2,300,000
Persons Served:			
Aged	4,500,000	4,900,000	5,100,000
Disabled		600,000	600,000

Eligibility: All persons aged 65 and over, who receive or are eligible for Social Security or railroad retirement cash payments, are eligible for Medi-

35

care. Also eligible are Social Security and railroad retirement survivors and dependents over 65, all other persons who reached age 65 prior to 1968, and most other persons who reached 65 prior to 1974. Also eligible are those disabled persons under 65 who have been entitled for at least two years to Social Security or railroad retirement benefits.

Cost:	1971	1975	1976
General Funds	$889,688,000	$529,353,000	$658,430,000
TOTAL (All Federal)	$5,639,478,000	$10,681,490,000	$12,573,956,000

Annual Growth: Average 1971–1976 = 24.59%.

Financing: All federal, primarily from trust fund filled by Social Security taxes, but also including general funds to cover costs for those not eligible for Social Security or railroad retirement cash payments.

Overlap: All other programs. For practical purposes, a person receiving Medicare would not also be receiving Medicaid since, if eligible for Medicaid, he would not need Medicare.

History: Enacted in 1965 as an amendment to the 1935 Social Security Act, this program represents the first infusion of general funds into Social Security. The rapid growth of the program is a major factor in Social Security's progress toward bankruptcy, and its spending policies have also contributed to the rise in general health care costs.

Program: MEDICARE (Social Security Supplementary Medical Insurance)

Benefits: Subsidized physician and other non-hospital-related medical care for the aged and disabled.

Control and Administration: Federal government: Department of Health, Education, and Welfare (Health Care Financing Agency).

Recipients:	1971	1975	1976
Persons Enrolled:			
Aged		21,500,000	22,000,000
	19,800,000		
Disabled		1,800,000	2,000,000
Persons Served:			
Aged		11,200,000	12,700,000
	10,300,000		
Disabled		1,400,000	1,300,000

Eligibility: All persons eligible for Medicare (Social Security Hospital Insurance) are also eligible for this program.

Cost:	1971	1975	1976
Total Program	$2,317,852,000	$4,251,476,000	$5,156,524,000
TOTAL: Welfare (All Federal)	$1,262,575,000	$2,435,129,000	$3,033,313,000

Annual Growth: Welfare component, average 1971–1976 = 28.05%.

Financing: This program is financed approximately 60% from federal general funds and 40% from "insurance" premiums paid by persons enrolled ($7.20 per person per month in 1976).

Overlap: All other programs. For practical purposes, a person eligible for Medicaid would choose not to participate in this program.

History: Enacted in 1965 as an amendment to the 1935 Social Security Act, this program breaks the Social Security pattern by not relying on Social Security taxes. It is composed of premiums from participants and welfare from federal general funds. The rapid growth and liberal spending policies of this program have contributed to the rise in general health care costs.

Program: COMMUNITY MENTAL HEALTH PROGRAM

Benefits: "Comprehensive mental health services" to low-income mentally handicapped persons through community mental health centers. These services are essentially the same as public assistance social services provided to welfare recipients who are not mentally handicapped.

Control: Federal government: Department of Health, Education, and Welfare (Alcohol, Drug Abuse, and Mental Health Administration).

Administration: State and local governments.

Recipients: Available data are too inconsistent and incomplete for reliable presentation.

Eligibility: All persons defined as "mentally handicapped" and living within the area of service of a community mental health center are eligible. Mostly low-income persons are served, because most centers are in low-income areas. Also, the Office of Management and Budget has designated this program as "desirable for joint funding," which means that state and local costs related to the recipients of this program, but not funded by it, can be made up by funds from other federal welfare programs. Thus, recipients of other welfare programs are actively recruited, virtually to the exclusion of anyone else.

Cost:	1971	1975	1976
Federal	$376,379,000	$554,944,000	$375,842,000
State and Local	$41,820,000	$369,963,000	$375,842,000
	(est)*	(est)*	(est)*
TOTAL	*$418,199,000*	*$924,907,000*	*$751,684,000*
	(est)**	(est)	(est)

Annual Growth: Average 1971–1976 = 15.95%.

Financing: Federal funding starts at 90%, but reduces by 10% per year until it reaches 50%. State and local governments must make up the remainder, and eventually must pay the entire cost of the program.

37

Overlap: All other programs.

History: Enacted in 1963 as a stimulus to states to move hospitalized mental patients into community living, the program was amended to expand services and the recipient population during the late '60s. Public dissatisfaction with the program, caused by inadequate supervision of mental patients in community settings, coupled with the gradual reduction of federal financing built into the sharing formulas, has resulted in a recent decline in federal and total program costs. However, state and local governments have had to pick up most of the fiscal slack because of politically undeniable demands for continued service by recipients and their sponsors.

*Estimates of state and local costs are based on 90% federal funding in 1971, 60% in 1976, and 50% in 1976. This is an admittedly gross estimate, but probably conservative, since it does not take into account instances of 100% local funding after the federal funding has ceased entirely.

**1971 costs do not include those identifiable as alcoholism and drug abuse treatment costs, although until 1972 these functions were part of the Community Mental Health Program.

Program: COMMUNITY DRUG ABUSE TREATMENT PROGRAM

Benefits: Treatment and rehabilitation services for drug-dependent low-income persons through community mental health centers.

Control: Federal government: Department of Health, Education, and Welfare (Alcohol, Drug Abuse, and Mental Health Administration).

Administration: State and local governments.

Recipients: Available data are too inconsistent and incomplete for reliable presentation.

Eligibility: Anyone addicted to or dependent on drugs and living within the area of service of a community mental health center is eligible. Mostly low-income persons are served, because most centers are in low-income areas. Also, the Office of Management and Budget has designated this program as "desirable for joint funding," which means that state and local costs related to the recipients of this program, but not funded by it, can be made up from other federal welfare programs. Thus, recipients of other welfare programs are actively recruited, virtually to the exclusion of anyone else.

Cost:	1971	1975	1976
Federal	$37,142,000	$283,434,000	$237,233,000
State and Local	$4,127,000	$188,956,000	$237,233,000
	(est)*	(est)*	(est)*
TOTAL	*$41,269,000*	*$472,390,000*	*$474,466,000*
	(est)**	(est)	(est)

Annual Growth: Average 1971–1976 = 209.94%.

38

Financing: Federal funding starts at 90%, but reduces by 10% per year until it reaches 50%. State and local governments must make up the remainder, and eventually must pay the entire cost of the program.

Overlap: All other programs.

History: This program was a small part of the Community Mental Health Program until 1972. Rapid initial growth has slowed somewhat due to lack of demonstrable success and the gradual reduction of federal funding built into the sharing formulas. State and local governments have had to pick up most of the fiscal slack because of politically undeniable demands for continued service by recipients and their sponsors.

*Estimates of state and local costs are based on 90% federal funding in 1971, 60% in 1975, and 50% in 1976. This is an admittedly gross estimate, but probably conservative, since it does not take into account instances of 100% local funding after the federal funding has ceased entirely.

**1971 costs are those identifiable as drug abuse treatment costs in the Community Mental Health Program for that year.

Program: COMMUNITY ALCOHOLISM TREATMENT PROGRAM

Benefits: Alcoholism treatment services, through community mental health centers, for low-income alcoholics and "problem drinkers" and their families.

Control: Federal government: Department of Health, Education, and Welfare (Alcohol, Drug Abuse, and Mental Health Administration).

Administration: State and local governments.

Recipients: Available data are too inconsistent and incomplete for reliable presentation.

Eligibility: All alcoholics and "problem drinkers" and their families living within the area of service of a community mental health center are eligible. Mostly low-income persons are served because most centers are in low-income areas. Also, the Office of Management and Budget has designated this program as "desirable for joint funding," which means that state and local costs related to the recipients of this program, but not funded by it, can be made up from other federal welfare programs. Thus, recipients of other welfare programs are actively recruited, virtually to the exclusion of anyone else.

Cost:	1971	1975	1976
Federal	$7,921,000	$207,824,000	$151,722,000
State and Local	$880,000	$138,540,000	$151,722,000
	(est)*	(est)*	(est)*
TOTAL	*$8,801,000*	*$346,373,000*	*$303,444,000*
	(est)**	(est)	(est)

39

Annual Growth: Average 1971–1976 = 669.57%.

Financing: All federal for demonstration grants. For remainder of program federal funding starts at 90%, but reduces by 10% per year until it reaches 50%. State and local governments must make up the remainder, and eventually must pay the entire cost of the program.

Overlap: All other programs.

History: This program was enacted in 1970, separated from the Community Mental Health Program in 1972, and augmented sharply in 1974 and 1975. Growth has now slowed because of lack of demonstrable success. Gradual reduction of federal funding is built into the sharing formulas, but state and local governments have had to pick up the fiscal slack because of politically undeniable demands for continued service by recipients and their sponsors.

*Estimates of state and local costs are based on 90% federal funding in 1971, 60% in 1975, and 50% in 1976. This is an admittedly gross estimate, but probably conservative, since it does not take into account instances of 100% local funding after the federal funding has ceased entirely.

**1971 costs are those identifiable as alcoholism treatment costs in the Community Mental Health Program for that year.

Cash Assistance Programs

Program: SOCIAL SECURITY OLD AGE AND SURVIVORS INSURANCE (OASI)

Benefits: Monthly cash payments to retired workers, their dependents, and their dependent survivors.

Control and Administration: Federal government: Department of Health, Education, and Welfare (Social Security Administration).

Recipients:	1971	1975	1976
Retired Workers	13,900,000	16,200,000	16,600,000
Dependents	3,200,000	3,500,000	3,600,000
Survivors	6,500,000	7,300,000	7,400,000
Total	23,600,000	26,900,000	27,500,000

Eligibility: Retired Workers aged 62 and over who have accumulated the required number of years (minimum of 10) of Social Security-taxed work, their dependents, and their dependent survivors are eligible. Dependents are defined as children under 18 (22 if in school) and spouses over 62 or with dependent children. Anyone over 72 is eligible, regardless of work experience.

Cost:	1971	1975	1976
Total (All Federal)	$32,651,164,000	$57,739,935,000	$65,232,090,000

WELFARE
COMPONENT $24,500,000,000 $43,300,000,000 $49,000,000,000
(est)* (est)* (est)*
Annual Growth: Welfare component, average 1971–1976 = 20%.

Financing: All federal, and virtually all from Social Security taxes on workers and employers, plus the interest derived from tax investment.

Overlap: All other programs, except Social Security Disability Insurance and Unemployment Insurance.

History: This program is the original, basic Social Security program enacted in 1935. Due to frequent amendments, most of them in election years, benefits, recipient population, and taxes have grown enormously, bringing the Social Security trust funds to the verge of bankruptcy.

*The author estimates that, in the 1971–1976 period, approximately 75% of OASDI costs are welfare, based on the more detailed calculations of Douglas R. Munro in his "Welfare Component and Labor Supply Effects of OASDHI Retirement Benefits" (Ph.D. dissertation, Ohio State University, 1976).

Program: SOCIAL SECURITY DISABILITY INSURANCE (DI)

Benefits: Monthly cash payments to disabled workers and their dependents.

Control and Administration: Federal government: Department of Health, Education, and Welfare (Social Security Administration).

Recipients:	1971	1975	1976
Disabled Workers	1,500,000	2,200,000	2,500,000
Dependents	1,200,000	1,700,000	1,900,000
Total	2,700,000	3,900,000	4,400,000

Eligibility: Disabled workers who have worked a sufficient amount of time in Social Security-taxed work (time varying with age) and their dependents are eligible. Dependents are defined as children under 18 (22 if in school), and spouses over 62 or with dependent children.

Cost:	1971	1975	1976
Total (All Federal)	$3,658,804,000	$8,062,408,000	$9,791,617,000
WELFARE COMPONENT	$2,750,000,000 (est)*	$6,050,000,000 (est)*	$7,350,000,000 (est)*

Annual Growth: Welfare component, average 1971–1976 = 33.45%.

Financing: All federal, and virtually all from Social Security taxes on workers and employers, plus the interest derived from Social Security tax investment.

41

Overlap: All other programs, except Social Security Old Age and Survivors Insurance and Unemployment Insurance. Also, benefits are reduced by the amount of any Workers Compensation benefits.

History: Disability benefits were added to the Social Security package in 1956 and, due to constant liberalization of the definition of "disabled," this part of Social Security has grown faster than Medicare in recent years. If the present rate of expenditures continues, this program's trust fund will be totally depleted in 1979.

*The author estimates that, in the 1971–1976 period, approximately 75% of OASDI costs are welfare, based on the more detailed calculations of Douglas R. Munro in his "Welfare Component and Labor Supply Effects of OASDHI Retirement Benefits" (Ph.D. dissertation, Ohio State University, 1976).

Program: SPECIAL BENEFITS FOR DISABLED COAL MINERS

Benefits: Monthly cash payments to coal miners disabled or killed by pneumoconiosis (black lung disease) and to their families and close relatives.

Control and Administration: Federal government: Department of Health, Education, and Welfare (Social Security Administration).

Recipients:	*1971*	*1975*	*1976*
Miners, Widows, Dependents, Relatives	198,000	507,000	500,000

Eligibility: Coal miners who are no longer physically able to work in the mines due to black lung disease, their widows, and their dependent children, parents, and brothers and sisters are eligible.

Cost:	*1971*	*1975*	*1976*
TOTAL (All Federal)	*$342,106,000*	*$966,018,000*	*$1,004,393,000*

Annual Growth: Average 1971–1976 = 38.72%.

Financing: All federal.

Overlap: All other programs. However, benefits under this program are reduced by the amount of any payments from Workers Compensation, Unemployment Insurance, or state disability insurance programs.

History: This program was enacted in 1969 to offset the income loss to coal miners of black lung disease. The growth of the recipient population has leveled off, but costs continue to rise far faster than the cost of living.

Program: SUPPLEMENTAL SECURITY INCOME (SSI)

Benefits: Monthly cash payments to adults who are aged, blind, or disabled. The payments provide a guaranteed minimum income, after certain deductions, of $157.70 for an individual and $236.60 for a couple, adjusted upward quarterly for cost of living increases after 1974. States provide supplemental payments to each recipient at least to the level of former state programs for the aged, blind, and disabled. The program also provides vocational rehabilitation services for potentially self-supporting blind and disabled recipients, and monitoring services for drug addicts and alcoholics eligible for the cash payments.

Control: Federal government: Department of Health, Education, and Welfare (Social Security Administration).

Administration: Federal government (Social Security Administration) and, for state supplements and at state option, state and local governments.

Recipients:	1971	1975	1976
Aged	2,059,502	2,013,000	1,961,000
Blind	79,905		1,917,000
		1,622,000	
Disabled	921,031		
State Supplements			430,000
Total	3,060,438	3,635,000	4,308,000

Eligibility: Low-income adults who are either over age 65 or medically certified as blind or permanently and totally disabled.

Cost:	1971	1975	1976
Federal	$2,302,380,000	$4,690,167,000	$5,031,859,000
State	$1,630,874,000	$1,243,938,000	$1,330,907,000
TOTAL	*$3,933,254,000*	*$5,934,105,000*	*$6,362,766,000*

Annual Growth: Average 1971–1976 = 12.35%.

Financing: The federal government pays all of the costs of the basic program, plus the administrative costs of state supplementation if administered by the federal government. States pay the remainder, and may pass some of the cost on to local government.

Overlap: All other programs, except programs exclusively for children.

History: This program was originally enacted, as a part of the Social Security Act of 1935, as two separate federal-state matching programs for the aged and blind. The disabled were added in 1957. These programs were combined into SSI in 1974, in part to gain more federal control of administration and in part to hide the incredible growth of the disabled program due to liberalized definitions of disability. The population of eligible disabled is growing at 15% to 20% per year, but since the number of aged recipients is slowly diminishing (principally due to greater Social Security coverage of the same population), the total SSI program does not appear to be growing rapidly. State costs were originally reduced by the 1974 SSI legislation, but are gradually rising again as federal administration makes more and more applicants eligible for disability payments.

Program: PUBLIC ASSISTANCE GRANTS (AFDC)

Benefits: Monthly cash payments to low-income families to "meet the costs of necessary items of daily living." Also emergency cash assistance.

Control: Federal government: Department of Health, Education, and Welfare (Social Security Administration).

Administration: State and local governments.

Recipients:	1971	1975	1976
Persons in Families Receiving Payments	9,315,113	11,080,000	11,557,942

Eligibility: Low-income single-parent families with dependent children under 18 (21 if in school) are eligible. Also eligible, in 25 states, are two-parent families in which the father is employed fewer than 100 hours per month. Determination of "need" for the payments is made by the individual states, based on income, family size, and local cost of living.

Cost:	1971	1975	1976
Federal	$3,240,291,000	$5,139,262,000	$5,803,023,000
State	$2,637,679,000	$4,393,934,000	$4,862,979,000
TOTAL	*$5,877,970,000*	*$9,533,196,000*	*$10,666,002,000*

Annual Growth: Average 1971–1976 = 16.29%.

Financing: The federal government pays 55% (nationwide average, varying from state to state) of the cash payments and 50% of state administrative costs. State and local governments pay the remainder.

Overlap: All other programs, except those exclusively for adults. Also, AFDC may not be paid to a family with an unemployed father if the father is eligible for Unemployment Compensation.

History: This program was enacted as part of the Social Security Act of 1935, and has been amended frequently to expand benefit levels and the eligible population. The period of greatest growth has been from 1960 to the present, and especially from 1967, when amendments were enacted to require states to deduct more than one-third of earned income in determining continuing eligibility for payments. This change has allowed families with gross incomes far above the poverty level to receive AFDC payments and, as a result, to qualify for other welfare programs.

Program: REFUGEE ASSISTANCE PROGRAMS

Benefits: Cash payments and health care and other services to Cuban, Cambodian, and Vietnamese refugees.

Control: Federal government: Department of Health, Education, and Welfare (Social Security Administration).

44

Administration: State and local governments.

Recipients:	1971	1975	1976
Cubans	77,700	69,000	66,000 (est)
Cambodians and Vietnamese		35,000 (est)	35,000 (est)
Total	77,700	104,000	101,000

Eligibility: Low-income Cuban refugees in alien status who are registered with the Cuban Refugee Center in Miami are eligible. Cambodian and Vietnamese refugees are eligible if they meet the public assistance requirements of the states in which they reside.

Cost:	1971	1975	1976
Cuban	$112,125,000	$84,236,000	$84,678,000
Cambodian and Vietnamese	N/Appl.	$130,435,000	$210,716,000
TOTAL (All Federal)	*$112,125,000*	*$214,671,000*	*$295,394,000*

Annual Growth: Average 1971–1976 = 32.69%.

Financing: All federal.

Overlap: Refugees are separately identified from other public assistance recipients so that states can obtain the 100% federal funding for them. Thus, there is no overlap with other cash assistance and health care programs, such as AFDC, SSI, and Medicaid. All other programs overlap.

History: The Cuban refugee program was enacted in 1962, the Cambodian and Vietnamese refugee program in 1975. Of the 462,000 Cuban refugees registered, approximately 15% now constitute a permanent welfare population of aliens. It is too early to tell if the same results will occur in the Cambodian and Vietnamese programs. The annual per-recipient costs of refugee assistance are among the highest of any single welfare program: $2,925 for every man, woman, and child in the program.

Program: GENERAL ASSISTANCE (General Relief)

Benefits: Cash payments for emergencies and subsistence maintenance, mainly to those low-income persons ineligible for federally-funded programs. Benefits vary widely among the states, but are generally lower than those of AFDC or SSI.

Control and Administration: State and local governments.

Recipients:	1971	1975	1976
Cases	566,000	692,000	750,000 (est)

45

| Persons | 982,000 | 1,200,000 | 1,300,000 |
| | | (est) | (est) |

Eligibility: Eligibility varies widely from state to state. The main criteria are demonstrable need and ineligibility for federally-funded assistance. A "case" may be a single individual, a couple, or a family with minor children.

Cost:	1971	1975	1976
TOTAL (State and Local)	$817,000,000	$1,345,000,000	$1,400,000,000
			(est)

Annual Growth: Average 1971–1975 = 16.16%.

Financing: All state and local. Proportions of each vary from state to state.

Overlap: All other programs except the federally-financed payment programs, AFDC and SSI, although in some states General Assistance emergency payments may overlap even those. For practical purposes, a Social Security recipient would be unlikely to be eligible for General Assistance because of income and other federal benefits.

History: State General Assistance laws typically date back to early statehood, with major amendments and revisions following federal enactment of Social Security and other public assistance programs. With a few exceptions (most notably New York) state General Assistance programs have proven less costly than federally-funded programs, both in per-recipient payments and in administration, although the effects of pressure from organized welfare lobbying groups can be seen in the recent pattern of cost growth.

Employment and Work Training Programs
Program: WORK INCENTIVE PROGRAM (WIN)

Benefits: Job training, child care and other social services, and reimbursement of work and training-related expenses for adults in AFDC families.

Control: Federal government: divided between Department of Labor (Employment and Training Administration) and Department of Health, Education, and Welfare (Assistant Secretary of Human Development Services).

Administration: Divided, in most states, between state departments of employment and welfare and, in some states, between state and local governments.

Recipients:	1971	1975	1976
Persons in Training	108,000	34,630	30,605
Children in Child Care	98,000	96,805	83,847

Eligibility: Adults in AFDC families. Fathers in two-parent AFDC families must register for and participate in WIN to assure continued AFDC eligibility.

Cost:	1971	1975	1976
Federal	$131,695,000	$350,019,000	$355,877,000
State	$14,633,000	$38,891,000	$39,542,000
	(est)*	(est)*	(est)*
TOTAL	*$146,328,000*	*$388,910,000*	*$395,419,000*
	(est)	(est)	(est)

Annual Growth: Average 1971–1976 = 33.18%.

Financing: The federal government pays 90% of all costs; state and local governments pay the remainder.

Overlap: All other programs, except other work training programs.

History: Enacted in 1967, WIN is designed to provide work training and experience to employable adults in AFDC families, in hopes that such services will lead to full-time permanent employment. No one has yet been able to credibly measure its impact, but most reports indicate that it does not work. Welfare professionals dislike its job orientation, and the divisions of responsibility at both federal and state levels have resulted in conflicts and disorder. 1976 costs are almost three times the costs of 1971 for fewer than one-third the number of trainees.

*Estimate based upon 10% non-federal sharing requirement.

Program: COMPREHENSIVE EMPLOYMENT AND TRAINING ASSISTANCE PROGRAM (CETA)

Components: Apprenticeship Outreach and Apprenticeship Training, Public Service Employment, National OJT, Summer Youth Employment, Temporary Employment Assistance.

Benefits: Federally-funded job training and jobs in public agencies for unemployed, underemployed, and "disadvantaged" persons.

Control: Federal government: Department of Labor (Employment and Training Administration).

Administration: The federal government directly administers portions of the program involving approximately one-fourth of the total funds; state and local governments administer the remainder.

Recipients: In 1976 the appropriated funds were intended to provide 2,500,000 year-round job and training positions and 900,000 summer jobs. Available data on performance are too inadequate and inconsistent for reliable presentation.

Eligibility: Persons defined by Department of Labor as economically disadvantaged, unemployed, and underemployed are eligible. Some of the components are specifically geared to youth and areas of high unemployment.

Cost:	1971	1975	1976
TOTAL (All Federal)	N/Appl.	$3,245,536,000	$4,982,036,000

Annual Growth: 1975–1976 = 53.5%.

Financing: All federal.

Overlap: All other programs except other job training programs and, during actual employment, Unemployment Compensation.

History: Except for Apprenticeship Training, which was enacted in the '30s, the components of this program are attempts to alleviate the unemployment effects of recent recessions. More than three-quarters of the funds go to state and local governments for decentralized programs. The remainder is retained by the federal government for employment and training of Indians, migrant and seasonal farm workers, people who don't speak English well, criminal offenders, and potentially delinquent youths.

Program: EMPLOYMENT SERVICE PROGRAM

Benefits: Free employment counseling and job search services for unemployed persons.

Control: Federal government: Department of Labor (Employment and Training Administration).

Administration: State employment agencies.

Recipients:	1971	1975	1976
Placements	6,897,000	4,172,000	4,242,000 (est)

Eligibility: Services are open to anyone who is unemployed, but emphasis is on services to low-income persons. First priority for job referrals goes to veterans.

Cost:	1971	1975	1976
TOTAL (All Federal)	$374,360,000	$477,170,000	$531,578,000

Annual Growth: Average 1971–1976 = 8.4%.

Financing: All federal, as grants to state employment agencies.

Overlap: All other programs.

History: Enacted in 1933, this program is the traditional one for unemployed job counseling. Participation in the program is required as a condition of receiving unemployment compensation. Numerous amendments over the years have created special sub-programs favoring "disadvantaged" groups (such as veterans, youth, and the handicapped) and concentrating efforts on special activities (such as training and temporary employment). These special sub-programs have diverted funds and attention from the program's main function—job-finding for the unemployed—

and the result has been decreased program effectiveness as measured by numbers of placements.

Program: JOB CORPS

Benefits: Intensive educational and vocational training for low-income school drop-out youths, through contract training centers. Participants receive free room and board, medical and dental care, work clothing, and cash allowances.

Control: Federal government: Department of Labor (Employment and Training Administration).

Administration: Public and private job training centers awarded contracts by the Department of Labor.

Recipients:	*1971*	*1975*	*1976*
Participants	42,600	45,799	64,700

Eligibility: Legal residents of the United States, aged 16 through 21, school drop-outs for three months or more, who are unable to find or hold an "adequate" job and are "underprivileged" and "in need of a change of environment."

Cost:	*1971*	*1975*	*1976*
TOTAL (All Federal)	$134,283,000	$210,382,000	$134,301,000

Annual Growth: Expenditures for 1978 are projected to be $487,000,000.

Financing: All federal, through two-year renewable contracts for reimbursable expenses, which include all benefits to "corpsmembers" and all operating expenses of the training centers. Yearly benefits to one "corpsmember" cannot exceed $6,900.

Overlap: Probably minimal, since most conceivable benefits are covered by this very generous program, but overlap is not prohibited.

History: Enacted in 1964, this program provides live-in job training accommodations for school drop-outs who have not yet found their niche in the nation's prison system. The program encourages dropping-out of school, since benefits are only available to those who do. Public dissatisfaction with the country club atmosphere of some of the training centers and with discrimination in favor of drop-outs caused some cut-back in funding in 1976, but renewed growth is projected in the current federal budget. A $6,900 per-recipient/per-year "limit" makes this the most generous single welfare program.

Program: COMMUNITY SERVICE EMPLOYMENT FOR OLDER AMERICANS

Benefits: Federally-funded part-time jobs in community service activities for unemployed low-income persons aged 55 and over.

Control: Federal government: Department of Labor (Employment and Training Administration).

Administration: Local public and non-profit private agencies contracting with Department of Labor to provide community service jobs.

Recipients:	*1971*	*1975*	*1976*
Persons in Jobs	N/Appl.	N/Avbl.	19,700

Eligibility: Unemployed low-income persons aged 55 and over.

Cost:	*1971*	*1975*	*1976*
TOTAL (All Federal)	N/Appl.	$9,325,000	$38,419,000

Annual Growth: 1975–1976 = 312%. Projected 1978 costs are $90,000,000.

Financing: All federal, through grants to local public and private agencies to create and pay for jobs.

Overlap: All other programs.

History: Enacted in 1973, this program, along with other programs for the aging, appears headed for spectacular growth.

Program: UNEMPLOYMENT COMPENSATION PROGRAM

Components: Federal-State Unemployment Insurance, Unemployment Compensation for Federal Civilian Employees, Trade Adjustment Assistance, Unemployment Compensation for Ex-Servicemen, Federal-State Extended Unemployment Compensation, and Emergency Extended Unemployment Compensation.

Benefits: Weekly cash payments, averaging 65% of previous net wages (varies widely from state to state and among levels of income), to members of the work force during periods of unemployment up to 39 weeks (65 weeks during the 1975–1976 recession).

Control: Shared between the federal government—Department of Labor (Employment and Training Administration)—and state governments. Both collect payroll taxes; the federal government controls Unemployment Trust Fund investments and disbursements to the states; the states determine the benefit levels.

Administration: State governments.

Recipients:	1971	1975	1976
Average Weekly Number of Beneficiaries	1,962,000	3,504,000	3,518,000

Eligibility: Members of the work force who are involuntarily unemployed, and who are able and available to work. The definition of what constitutes "involuntary unemployment" varies from state to state.

Cost:	1971	1975	1976
Unemployment Trust Fund (Federal and State)	$6,025,806,000	$13,317,122,000	$17,686,124,000
Other (Federal)	$806,885,000	$1,494,032,000	$2,815,226,000
TOTAL	*$6,832,691,000*	*$14,631,154,000*	*$20,501,350,000*

Annual Growth: Average 1971–1976 = 40.0%.

Financing: The bulk of the financing is from the Unemployment Trust Fund, made up of federal and state unemployment insurance payroll taxes on employers plus investment interest. The lion's share of the taxes (72% in 1971, 84% in 1976) are collected by the states, but the federal government controls trust fund investments, and augments the trust fund with contributions from general funds for former federal employees, workers unemployed because of international trade concessions, and others not eligible for the state programs.

Overlap: All other programs, except that AFDC may not be paid to a family with an unemployed father if the father is eligible for unemployment compensation.

History: Enacted in 1935, the program has been amended frequently, especially during periods of high unemployment, to expand eligibility and increase the amount of benefits and length of benefit period.

Program: RAILROAD UNEMPLOYMENT COMPENSATION

Benefits: Cash payments to railroad workers who are sick or unemployed. Payments are 60% or more of claimant's regular wages, and each claimant is eligible for 130 compensable days each year, although compensation in a year may not exceed earnings from actual work in that year.

Control and Administration: Federal government: Railroad Retirement Board.

Recipients:	1971	1975	1976
Beneficiaries	170,000	145,000	200,000 (est)

Eligibility: Railroad workers who are unemployed or unable to work because of illness or injury, and who have earned at least $1,000 in the past year in the railroad industry, are eligible.

Cost:	1971	1975	1976
TOTAL (All Federal)	*$106,361,000*	*$74,001,000*	*$266,735,000*

Annual Growth: Average 1971–1976 = 30.16%.

51

Financing: The financing mechanism is the Railroad Unemployment Insurance Administration Fund, made up of tax receipts from a federal payroll tax on railroads plus investment interest.

Overlap: All other programs, except that benefits of this program may supplement, but not duplicate, benefits received from Social Security or Workers Compensation.

History: Enacted in 1938, the program has been amended several times to expand eligibility and benefits to parallel the more general Unemployment Compensation Program. The costs more than doubled between 1971 and 1976, although the eligible workforce shrank by 20%.

Program: WORKERS COMPENSATION PROGRAMS

Benefits: Cash subsistence and medical payments for workers injured on the job, and, if they are killed on the job, for their survivors. Benefits vary widely from state to state. Subsistence payments range from 50% to 90% of prior wages, and average 66%. Maximum payment periods range from 208 weeks to duration of disability without regard to length of time.

Control and Administration: Federal government for federal employees and some miners and longshoremen; state governments for everyone else.

Recipients: Available data are too inadequate and inconsistent for reliable presentation.

Eligibility: Any worker who suffers a job-related illness or injury resulting in temporary or permanent, partial or total disability, or who dies as a result of job-related illness or injury, is eligible for benefits. Injury or death as a result of a worker's gross negligence generally excludes that worker from benefits, but "gross negligence" is extremely difficult to prove. Virtually the entire labor force is now covered by these programs.

Cost:	1971	1975	1976
Federal	$148,000,000	$1,355,000,000	$2,000,000,000 (est)
State	$2,803,000,000	$5,082,000,000	$6,000,000,000 (est)
TOTAL	*$2,951,000,000*	*$6,437,000,000*	*$8,000,000,000* (est)

Annual Growth: Average 1971–1975 = 29.53%.

Financing: The federal government finances its own program from general revenues, with minor reimbursements from employers of longshoremen and coal miners, some of whom are covered by the federal program. All other workers are covered by state programs, which are financed by "insurance" taxes charged to employers based on payroll and disability experience.

Overlap: All other programs, although Workers Compensation payments may, in some states, be counted as income in determining AFDC or SSI benefit levels.

History: Workers Compensation programs have been enacted at various times, state by state, until now all 50 states have one. They have been frequently amended, by law or interpretation, to expand eligibility and benefits. In the past few years Workers Compensation referees and, upon appeal, court judges, have begun to award benefits for "cumulative disability," in addition to outright illness and injury. Thus, a 20-year clerk-typist may become eligible for benefits for "cumulative backstrain," even though able to work until retirement. This novel interpretation has led to spiraling program costs and consequent increases in employer "insurance" rates. In some states, private insurance carriers act as agents of the state in administering Workers Compensation.

Education Programs

Program: FINANCIAL ASSISTANCE FOR ELEMENTARY AND SECONDARY EDUCATION (including Education for the Handicapped)

Benefits: Federal grants to states and local educational agencies to provide educational advantages for poor, handicapped, and other "disadvantaged" children.

Control: Federal government: Department of Health, Education, and Welfare (Education Division).

Administration: States through local public and private educational agencies.

Recipients: Current estimates of children "advantaged" by this program range from 5,000,000 to 10,000,000.

Eligibility: Basic grants are awarded to local school districts on the basis of how many children in the district are below the poverty level, in welfare families, or "disadvantaged" in some other economic sense. Special grants are awarded for handicapped children and special programs, such as bilingual education.

Cost:	1971	1975	1976
TOTAL (All Federal)	$1,712,687,000	$2,377,294,000	$2,450,764,000

Annual Growth: Average 1971–1976 = 8.62%.

Financing: All federal. The amount of each grant to a school district is based on a formula tied to the state's average per-pupil expenditure and the number of "disadvantaged" children in the district.

Overlap: All other programs. "Disadvantaged" children in this program are not excluded from participation in any other welfare program.

53

History: Enacted in 1965 as a supplement to state and locally-funded public education, and to private school financing, for children defined as "educationally deprived," the program has become a determinant of how lower education is conducted at the local level.

Program: FINANCIAL ASSISTANCE FOR HIGHER EDUCATION

Benefits: Federal grants and loans, based on financial need, to college students for up to one-half of college costs. Also grants to colleges and universities to encourage higher participation of minorities and community service programs.

Control: Federal government: Department of Health, Education, and Welfare (Education Division).

Administration: Participating colleges and universities administer student grants and loans. The federal government administers the grants to colleges and universities for other elements of the program.

Recipients:	1971	1975	1976
Number of Students Receiving:*			
Basic Opportunity Grants	N/Appl.	600,000	1,268,300
Supplemental Grants	290,500	393,000	447,000
Work-Study Grants	430,000	626,000	973,000
Subsidized Loans	1,087,000	874,000	923,000
Direct Loans	560,400	674,000	799,000
Incentive Grants for State Scholarships	N/Appl.	76,000	80,000

*Numbers do not total due to overlap among programs.

Eligibility: College and university students who can demonstrate financial need either as independent individuals or as members of families which cannot afford the costs of higher education. Need is determined by the college or university based on a needs analysis program approved annually by the Congress.

Cost:	1971	1975	1976
Basic and Supplemental Grants		$413,946,000	$1,213,647,000
Work-Study Grants	$721,643,000	$300,175,000	$524,968,000
Individual Loans		$697,341,000	$602,579,000
Other Costs	$93,248,000	$330,767,000	$248,823,000
TOTAL (All Federal)	$814,891,000	$1,742,229,000	$2,590,017,000

Annual Growth: Average 1971–1976 = 43.57%.

Financing: All federal, except that work-study grants must be matched 30% by the receiving educational institution. In 1976 this match would amount to about 5% of the total program.

Overlap: All other programs, although work-study grants may, in some states, be counted as earned income, and thus may reduce AFDC payments.

History: The bulk of this program was enacted in 1965, with important amendments in 1969. In the past five years it has revolutionized the financing of higher education by forcing institutions to construct individual education financing packages—consisting of a mix of grants, loans, and jobs—for almost all students. The program has undoubtedly contributed heavily to the rapid rise of higher education costs. The most controversial part of the program is the federally insured (subsidized) loan portion. Defaults on repayment of these loans by college graduates and drop-outs currently total $400,000,000, constituting a debt to the federal government.

Service and Miscellaneous Programs

Program: PUBLIC ASSISTANCE SERVICES (AFDC)

Benefits: A wide range of social services, including day care, foster child care, child protection, child support enforcement, and family planning, for AFDC cash payment recipients and former and potential recipients.

Control: Federal government: Department of Health, Education, and Welfare (Assistant Secretary for Human Development).

Administration: State and local governments.

Recipients: Current estimates of persons receiving services range from 12,000,000 to 15,000,000.

Eligibility: Persons who are members of a current, former, or potential AFDC family, and who have a need for service, are eligible.

Cost:	1971	1975	1976
Federal	$791,490,000	$2,087,825,000	$2,286,551,000
State	$720,992,000 (est)*	$1,224,098,000	$1,415,064,000
TOTAL	*$1,512,482,000* (est)	*$3,311,923,000*	*$3,701,615,000*

Annual Growth: Average 1971–1976 = 28.95%.

Financing: Federal financial participation varies from about 7% for child welfare services to 100% for research and training projects. Most other services are 75% federally financed, except family planning at 90%. State and local governments pay the remainder.

Overlap: All other programs.

History: Social services have been an adjunct to the public assistance payment programs (AFDC and SSI) since 1956. The rapid growth rate of service costs in the past ten years is due primarily to amendments and regulations which have extended eligibility beyond that of the payment programs (to former and "potential" payment recipients) and to increased emphasis on services to allow women to leave the home, such as day care and family planning.

*In the absence of reliable data, the state and local share of the child welfare component of this program has been estimated by the author to be $475,000,000. Actual comparable figures for 1975 and 1976 are, respectively, $498,320,000 and $700,059,000.

Program: HUMAN DEVELOPMENT SERVICES

Components: Head Start, Vocational Rehabilitation, Programs for the Aging.

Benefits: Assorted development services for low-income aged and disabled persons and children. Provides pre-school training through Head Start, meals and community services for the aged, and vocational rehabilitation for the handicapped.

Control: Federal government: Department of Health, Education, and Welfare (Assistant Secretary for Human Development).

Administration: State and local governments.

Recipients:	*1971*	*1975*	*1976*
Child Development Participants	N/Avbl.	350,000 (est)	340,000 (est)
Active Rehabilitation Cases	1,001,660	1,224,000	1,300,000 (est)
Number of Aged Served	N/Avbl.	Approximately 250,000	

Eligibility: Theoretically open to anyone, but with practical limitations which limit participation almost exclusively to low-income persons. Head Start requires that at least 80% of its participants come from low-income families. Both the rehabilitation programs for the handicapped and the nutrition program for the aging have been designated by the Office of Management and Budget as "desirable for joint funding." This means that state and local costs related to the recipients of these programs, but not funded by them, can be made up by funds from other federal welfare programs. Thus, recipients of other welfare programs are recruited, virtually to the exclusion of anyone else.

56

Cost:	1971	1975	1976
Child Development	$450,094,000	$585,388,000	$540,748,000
Rehabilitation	$670,480,000	$911,610,000	$978,695,000
Aging	$33,371,000	$306,560,000	$326,148,000
Total Federal	$925,555,000	$1,455,168,000	$1,492,134,000
Total State	$228,390,000	$348,390,000	$353,457,000
TOTAL	$1,153,945,000	$1,803,558,000	$1,845,591,000

Annual Growth: Average 1971–1976 = 11.99%.

Financing: With a few small exceptions, costs of these services are 80% federally funded, with state and local governments paying the remainder.

Overlap: All other programs.

History: The child development components of this program date from 1969; in 1971 Head Start was still a small experimental program. The rehabilitation components were first enacted in 1935 as part of the Social Security Act. They have been amended to expand benefits and to include the mentally as well as the physically handicapped. The Older Americans Act of 1965 initiated the components for the aging. Control and direction of all of these components were centralized in a new HEW office in 1974.

Program: ACTION DOMESTIC PROGRAMS

Benefits: A potpourri of services to the poor performed by paid and unpaid volunteers. Includes the VISTA program.

Control and Administration: Federal government: ACTION, the federal agency for volunteer service.

Recipients: Available data are too inadequate and inconsistent for reliable presentation.

Eligibility: Anyone who appears poor enough to warrant the interest of an ACTION volunteer. Most of the efforts are focused on groups and communities, rather than on individuals.

Cost:	1971	1975	1976
TOTAL (All Federal)	$49,645,000	$100,907,000	$99,815,000

Annual Growth: Average 1971–1976 = 20.21%.

Financing: All federal.

Overlap: All other programs.

History: Most of these volunteer programs, such as VISTA, were initiated in the early '60s, when the Kennedy Administration was trying to find some way to circumvent the welfare and local government establishments in dealing with poverty problems. Voluntarism has made good rhetoric but poor programs, principally because of extremely critical treatment by professionals in the welfare industry.

Program: LEGAL SERVICES PROGRAM

Benefits: Federally-financed free legal advice and representation for low-income persons in non-criminal proceedings. Also education of the poor as to their legal rights.

Control: Federal government: Legal Services Corporation.

Administration: Local and regional public and private non-profit agencies contracting with Legal Services Corporation to provide legal services to the poor.

Recipients: Available data are too inconsistent and inadequate for reliable presentation.

Eligibility: Determined on a case by case basis by the agencies which contract with Legal Services Corporation to provide the service. The heaviest efforts of these agencies have been devoted to class-action suits affecting large groups of low-income persons.

Cost:	1971	1975	1976
TOTAL (All Federal)	$61,849,000	$71,499,000	$92,330,000

Annual Growth: Average 1971–1976 = 9.86%.

Financing: All federal.

Overlap: All other programs. Participation in this program does not affect eligibility for any other program.

History: Originally developed in the early '60s as a program in the Office of Economic Opportunity, legal services for the poor became the sole mission of the Legal Services Corporation, an independent agency formed in 1976. The program has been extremely controversial, principally because of its emphasis on class-action suits asking for the expenditure of large sums of government money to right supposed welfare injustices. In Legal Services Corporation-sponsored suits against the government, taxpayers find themselves in the no-win position of paying the legal fees of both plaintiff and defendant.

Program: VETERANS BENEFIT PROGRAMS

Benefits: A wide variety of payments and services to veterans of United States military service. Includes pensions and compensation for disabilities to ex-servicemen and their survivors; pensions based on need for wartime veterans with non-service-connected total disabilities; free medical care for aged veterans and those with service-connected disabilities; subsidized education, subsidized life insurance, and low-interest mortgage loans.

Control and Administration: Federal government: Veterans Administration.

Recipients:	1971	1975	1976
Veterans Potentially Eligible for Some or All Benefits	28,288,000	29,459,000	29,700,000
Pensioners	4,807,000	4,853,000	4,859,000
Medical Care Patients	3,790,000 (est)	5,600,000 (est)	6,100,000 (est)
Education Beneficiaries	1,585,000	2,692,000	2,822,000
Mortgage Borrowers	198,000	290,000	329,000

Eligibility: All veterans of United States military service and their dependents are potentially eligible for some veterans' benefits. Specific eligibility requirements vary from benefit to benefit. All veterans are eligible for low-interest mortgage loans for a home or farm, and all are eligible for educational assistance for a period of time following their release from active duty. Veterans over 65 and those with service-connected disabilities are eligible for free medical care in VA facilities. Those retired for service-connected disabilities are automatically eligible for pensions and compensation, while those wartime veterans who suffer a non-service-connected total disability are also eligible for pensions based on need.

Cost:	1971	1975	1976
Pensions and Compensation	$5,840,941,000	$7,544,382,000	$8,238,831,000
Readjustment (Education)	$1,626,171,000	$4,432,691,000	$5,333,633,000
Medical Care	$1,981,084,000	$3,425,712,000	$3,937,091,000
Other	$307,804,000	$1,322,215,000	$1,319,280,000
TOTAL (Federal Outlay)	*$9,756,000,000*	*$16,725,000,000*	*$18,414,835,000*

Annual Growth: Average 1971–1976 = 17.75%.

Financing: All federal.

Overlap: All other programs, except that pension and compensation income may be counted as unearned income in determining eligibility for AFDC, SSI, Medicaid, and Food Stamps. Also, participation in a VA mortgage loan may remove participant from eligibility for housing assistance programs.

History: The War Risk Insurance Act of 1917 established pensions and compensation for disabilities. Frequent amendments have extended eligibility and increased benefits. Medical care for veterans was enacted in

1930, and frequent amendments have also extended its scope and benefit level. Educational benefits were a feature of the G.I. Bill from World War II, and have been extended to all veterans since then. Life insurance subsidization has been in effect since World War I.

Program: INDIAN BENEFIT PROGRAMS

Components: Programs of the Bureau of Indian Affairs, Indian Education, Indian Health Services, Indian Health Facilities, and Special (Development) Program for Native Americans.

Benefits: A wide range of education, health, and welfare services for American Indians, including Eskimos.

Control and Administration: Federal government: Department of the Interior (Bureau of Indian Affairs) and Department of Health, Education, and Welfare (Education Division, Health Services Administration, and Assistant Secretary for Human Development).

Recipients: Estimates of numbers of persons receiving benefits from these programs in 1976 vary from 450,000 to 550,000.

Eligibility: A person's eligibility for these programs depends upon recognition as an Indian by the Bureau of Indian Affairs. Persons acknowledged as members or spouses of members by recognized tribes are assured eligibility.

Cost:	1971	1975	1976
Bureau of Indian Affairs (Outlay)	$463,919,000	$865,254,000	$902,805,000
Indian Education	N/Appl.	$41,963,000	$33,484,000
Indian Health	$150,075,000	$285,998,000	$327,659,000
Special Native American Program	N/Appl.	$32,276,000	$33,143,000
TOTAL (All Federal)	*$613,994,000*	*$1,225,491,000*	*$1,297,091,000*

Annual Growth: Average 1971–1976 = 22.25%.

Financing: All federal.

Overlap: These programs mainly serve Indians living on reservations not served by most other welfare programs. Benefit levels of $2,500 to $3,000 per-person per-year, combined with the wealth of many tribes, probably make overlap with other programs a relatively rare occurrence.

History: These programs have grown out of an Indian assistance law passed in 1921. The Department of the Interior was assigned responsibility for them in 1934. In 1954 Indian Health was transferred to the Department of Health, Education, and Welfare. Indian Education and the Special Program for Native Americans originated in that department in the early '70s in response to Indian dissatisfaction with the Bureau of Indian Affairs.

60

Program: COMMUNITY SERVICES PROGRAMS

Components: Community Action, Community Economic Development, Community Food and Nutrition, Older Persons Opportunities and Services.

Benefits: A variety of services to stimulate community economic, educational, and social activities involving low-income persons and families.

Control: Federal government: Community Services Administration.

Administration: Local Community Action Agencies under contract to CSA.

Recipients: Available data are too inconsistent and incomplete for reliable presentation.

Eligibility: There are no uniform eligibility requirements, although local Community Action Agencies normally use the federally-defined poverty level as a guideline for participation.

Cost:	1971	1975	1976
Federal	$578,648,000*	$521,975,000	$518,650,000
State and Local	N/Appl.	$82,500,000	$131,500,000
TOTAL	*$578,648,000*	*$604,475,000*	*$650,150,000*

Annual Growth: 2.47%.

Financing: All federal until 1974, when the federal government established a sharing formula designed to turn financing over to the states and local governments. In 1975 the non-federal share was 20% for Community Action Agencies. In 1976 the share was raised to 25% for agencies spending less than $300,000, 30% for agencies spending more than $300,000.

Overlap: All other programs.

History: These programs are the principal remnants of the Office of Economic Opportunity, organized in the early '60s in an attempt to circumvent state and local government in the handling of poverty problems. The recent federal requirement for local funding has slowed the growth of these programs to a virtual standstill.

*Funding level for corresponding programs in Office of Economic Opportunity budget for 1971.

3

Organization of the Welfare Industry

Industry Goals

The national welfare system had its inception in federal programs set up during the depression of the 1930s to alleviate the poverty caused by widespread unemployment and the failure of pensions and other investments. Federal welfare was designed as a temporary expedient and it was commonly believed that as the economy improved the need would decrease, if not to nothing, at least to a level of minor supplementation of other income sources.[39]

Before 1935, welfare had been almost exclusively the province of local governments and private charities. Efforts were concentrated on increasing self-reliance and reducing dependency and the need for welfare. Welfare administrators were neighbors both of those who paid for it and those who received it, and clearly the less needed the better.

But federal welfare programs spawned a national welfare industry, led by federal bureaucrats far removed from local pressures to contain welfare spending.[40] Reducing dependency on government welfare was not in their self-interest.[41] Their careers depended on more people becoming more dependent, and thus they set expansionary goals for the welfare industry.

The first of these goals is to make welfare a growth industry; that is, to produce a continuous growth of welfare expenditures at a pace greater than national economic growth. The industry has rationalized this goal by defining poverty as "need," and has met the goal by periodically escalating the levels of "need" defined in welfare law and regulation. Defining a higher level of "need" automatically makes more people eligible for welfare, and at the same time creates pressures for higher benefits for those already eligible. In effect, "need" has been made synonymous with "demand" in the welfare industry, and control of the definition of "need" is control of production and industry growth.

The inherent subjectivity of any definition of "need," and the industry's recognition that the definition could best be controlled for growth if it issued from a godhead, led to the goal of centralizing control and administration of welfare programs at the federal level. This goal has been rationalized on the basis that there should be nationwide uniformity in welfare

63

policies and benefits, and that the states cannot provide such uniformity. For years the national "oracle" for determining nationwide "need" has been housed in HEW, and every major revision of welfare laws has used federally defined "need" as a rationale for increasing federal control of policy and administration.[42]

The third goal of the welfare industry is to make the welfare system increasingly complex, for complexity eases the task of system control and expansion in the face of fluctuating political pressures. With federal laws governing 42 of the 44 welfare programs, the only potential deterrent to growth is an informed Congress, acting in response to public dissatisfaction with welfare costs. By complicating the design of welfare programs the industry has made the system extremely difficult for Congress to understand. Moreover, most members of Congress have been reluctant to become "experts" on welfare because of the political unpopularity of welfare in the public eye.[43] As a result, Congress has come to rely on industry experts for judgments about welfare legislation, and the experts have furthered their own and the industry's interests by fostering complexity.

The fourth goal of the welfare industry is to create jobs for people in the industry. Emphasis on this goal in the past 15 years has resulted in an explosive increase in service programs as compared to programs providing cash assistance. The rationalization for service instead of cash is that poor people do not spend money intelligently and that it is better for society if the government spends it for them. By promoting service programs, the industry has taken direct control of a greater proportion of welfare expenditures,[44] increased industry job opportunities, and made itself the principal market for a number of service trades, especially in the health care field.[45]

Organizational Structure

The organization of the welfare industry is, like the welfare system itself, complex. Decisions are made informally,[46] in an atmosphere of philosophical agreement with industry goals. Thus, the organization is, like a half-filled balloon with a very tough skin, virtually impenetrable. Outsiders, including many of the nation's political leaders, are uncertain about who belongs to it and who controls it, since its products seldom leave a clear audit trail. Insiders often know less; they shift positions rapidly and there is seldom any tacit acknowledgement either of good or bad performance. There is no conspiracy to control, only a common commitment to self-interest.

HEW is the acknowledged headquarters of the industry. It controls two-fifths of the national welfare programs and three-fifths of national welfare expenditures.[47] Welfare constitutes 80 percent of the entire HEW budget.[48]

64

Potentially, then, the single most powerful position in the industry is that of the Secretary of HEW, but most of its occupants have not been able to exploit that potentiality. There have been 12 appointees to the position since the department was formed in 1953.[49] Those in substantial sympathy with industry goals have helped push industry programs,[50] while the others have been content to administer the department and its programs without disturbing either. None, while in office, has publicly questioned the growth of the welfare system or the goals of the industry.[51]

The true force of HEW's industry leadership is exerted away from the public eye, at the lower appointed levels and at the higher non-appointed levels. These middle management positions are occupied mainly by persons who equate the growth of the welfare system with the furtherance of their careers, since they are either the more successful members of the civil service or appointees who were selected because they are "technically qualified"; that is, identified with past industry developments.[52]

It is at these levels that program and budget decisions are formulated, justified, and packaged for sale to the Cabinet, the President, Congress, and the public.[53] And it is here that regulations are prepared to control welfare administration by the states.

HEW's regulatory control of state welfare agencies has a double benefit: it keeps the states in line and provides a minor league training ground for future HEW leaders. State and local welfare managers who demonstrate their support of industry goals are a major source of reliable talent for appointments to HEW positions.[54]

Another source of talent is the congressional staff. Many staff members are brought to Washington D.C. on a temporary basis by members of Congress. Those who wish to stay in Washington, and who are willing to espouse welfare industry goals, become the needed allies of the bureaucracy in proposing welfare legislation and justifying budget requests. Having proven trustworthy, they can look forward to careers in the executive branch or on the staffs of a succession of congressmen friendly to the welfare industry.

Three other federal departments—Agriculture, HUD, and Labor— manage several welfare programs each. These departments follow generally the HEW model of middle management control, with more emphasis on federal, as opposed to state, administration. They compete with HEW and with each other for appropriations for new and expanded programs, but close ranks quickly when an industry-wide threat or opportunity arises.[55]

Five other federal agencies control only one welfare program each. The Veterans Administration and the Department of Interior's Bureau of Indian Affairs serve special populations, and normally involve themselves with industry-wide matters only when the programs of multi-program departments impinge on those populations. Both of these agencies are relatively parochial, aloof, and reluctant to recognize themselves as part of the welfare system. The Community Services Administration, the Legal Services Corporation, and ACTION are remnants of the Johnson Administration's "War on Poverty." Bred on theories of confrontation, these agencies manage small, controversial programs outside the mainstream of the industry, and often find themselves more criticized by industry leaders than by industry critics.[56] While these agencies support industry goals, their radical reputations exclude them from serious involvement in industry policymaking.

Philosophical support of industry goals, and technical support of industry programs and the federal departments that run them is provided by friendly congressmen and by universities, consultants, and profit and non-profit firms seeking or performing government grants and contracts. Columbia University's School of Social Work, the University of Wisconsin's Institute for Research on Poverty, and the University of Michigan's Institute for Social Research have been particularly influential in policy research and development.[57] The Brookings Institution in Washington, D.C. has been a consistent apologist for expansionary welfare policies and budgets.[58] Mathematica, Inc., has provided elaborate computer-based statistical support for HEW program assessments and proposals.[59]

Welfare employees' unions,[60] welfare rights organizations,[61] "minority" organizations,[62] and many state and local welfare agencies[63] also actively support industry goals, although their specialized interests sometimes conflict with the program management plans of the federal agencies that control the industry.[64] The industry uses them selectively for support, particularly in lobbying Congress.

How the Organization Works

The middle management of HEW and other federal departments controls the welfare industry by design and default. By design, the welfare system has been placed under federal control, through laws that require "top-down" policy development and administrative regulation. By default of members of Congress and top-level appointees in the executive branch, the exercise of that control has fallen to middle management, a group with no constituency, little competition, and a common loyalty only to the welfare industry goals that will further their careers.

How these middle managers exercise control, with the support of the rest of the industry, is best illustrated by examining the processes related to program changes and budget allocations.

Innovation seldom originates in the bureaucracy; the ideas for program change come mainly from outside sources: universities, Congress, even the

66

press. How much consideration the bureaucracy gives to an idea for change depends on the political appeal of the idea and the political strength of its originator. But all ideas are subjected to the same filtering and altering process—a process guaranteed to make any program change conform to welfare industry goals.

The process consists of fitting those goals—expansion, complexity, centralization, and employment for welfare workers—to the idea, and bending the idea wherever it doesn't fit. It is an informal process, accomplished quietly and with low visibility in the federal agencies, through discussions, briefings, memos, and work sessions. Occasionally a formal analysis of some technical question is contracted-out to a friendly research firm. Usually several ideas are blended into a larger proposal to disguise the extent to which any one of the ideas is being altered to satisfy the industry.

During this process the position of the idea's author—be he an academician, a member of Congress, or even the President—is awkward indeed.[65] He has turned his idea over to the experts, who are analyzing its virtues and potential for implementation. From time to time he meets with them, and they suggest minor changes to make his idea more "implementable" (if the author is a member of Congress) or "saleable" (if he is not), or who show him how they are blending his idea with others to make up a package which is more "saleable" or "implementable." The experts are always solicitous of his judgment and anxious to secure his concurrence that they are still on the right track.

When the experts unveil the "program" that his idea has become, it is so complex that he really cannot tell if it will do what he wanted it to. The fact that his idea is still there, even though modified and buried in confusing procedures, is usually enough to get his approval. Having been made part of the process of converting his idea to a program acceptable to the welfare industry, later he finds it both difficult and ineffective to complain when the program doesn't meet his original expectations.

Some of the more experienced members of Congress have tried to avoid this metamorphosing process by designing programs without the help of the bureaucracy, only to find that the process is applied anyway—after the program is enacted into law. Through implementing regulations and other administrative directives, the agencies either make the law unworkable or bend it to meet welfare industry goals.[66]

Expansionary budget requests are a more difficult problem to the industry, a problem requiring a more direct and definitive solution. The Congress, prompted and supported by the Office of Management and Budget, is theoretically capable of setting expenditure limits on welfare programs, and thus reducing industry growth. Public pressure to do just that has made the threat a serious one.

67

The industry has laid to rest this specter of "controlled growth" by developing, with the help of the Brookings Institution and non-welfare segments of the federal bureaucracy, the concept of "uncontrollable expenditures."[67] The concept justifies the politically appealing notion that most government growth is the result of past decisions, and therefore cannot be modified by or blamed on the current President and Congress.

"Uncontrollable expenditures" are those which ostensibly cannot be controlled through the budgetary process, either because they are prior contractual obligations of government or because they are mandated by law.[68] In 1976, 90 percent of the non-defense budget, including virtually all welfare, was deemed "uncontrollable," and therefore beyond the reach of would-be budget cutters.[69] Presidents Ford and Carter and the last two Congresses have supported the concept.

Taking advantage of the rhetoric of its own splinter groups, the industry has also fostered the theory that, in fact, the Constitution and federal law mandate ever-increasing welfare expenditures. Welfare rights groups and Legal Services Corporation attorneys have attempted to make the case that welfare benefits, once enacted in law, become welfare rights that cannot be revoked. If this is true then, by extension, as long as there are people who can be defined by the federal government as living "in poverty," welfare expenditures must constantly be increased. The industry has used this argument to bring political pressure on Congress not to reduce previously-granted benefits, and thus has blunted attempts to reform the welfare system through redefinition of "need."[70]

4

Welfare Reform

The Public vs. the Welfare Industry

Welfare reform is a political idea, created in response to dissatisfaction with the welfare system. There are major gaps between the way the system operates and the way the public thinks it should operate. Opinion surveys indicate public desire for reforms to eliminate cheaters, cut costs, provide adequate aid to those who can't work, require work of those who can, and simplify the distribution of benefits.[71] The key issue of welfare reform is the conflict between work and welfare, personified by the resentment of the tax-paying worker toward his welfare-collecting neighbor.

The welfare industry has its own agenda for reform, one more closely aligned to industry goals. Table 5 summarizes the contrasts between public and industry reform ideas.

TABLE 5
Contrast of Public and Industry Welfare Reform Ideas

Public Reform Ideas	Industry Reform Ideas
Eliminate Cheaters	Reduce Fraud
Cut Costs	Increase Costs
Provide Adequate Aid to Those Who Can't Work	Expand Welfare Benefits and Population
Require Work of Those Who Can	Provide Work with Welfare
Simplify System	Complicate System

To the taxpaying public, welfare is a privilege, not a right, and anyone who takes more than he needs is a "cheater." Among the "cheaters" are those who take welfare instead of working, those who work and also get welfare, and those who get welfare despite the availability of other financial resources.[72] Because of the way the industry has designed its programs, the vast majority of these "cheaters" are legally entitled to welfare, and even encouraged by the government to obtain it. The industry's corresponding reform idea is to eliminate only those who are not legally entitled to welfare and who have lied in attempts to get it. The number of those committing fraud to get welfare is, of course, only a small fraction of the number of those who, in the opinion of the public, are "cheaters."[73]

69

The public is poorly informed about overall welfare costs, since the information it receives almost always relates to only one or a few programs, and thus understates the costs of the system. Even major reform proposals cover only a portion of the system. The Carter-Califano plan covers only 20 percent of national welfare expenditures;[74] the Nixon Family Assistance Plan of several years ago covered even less.[75] The welfare industry studiously avoids publishing total system costs and cost growth rates. Nevertheless, the public, even on limited information, firmly believes that too much money is being spent on welfare.[76] Yet every proposal produced or endorsed by the industry has included increased welfare spending, and the industry has consistently fought proposals designed to cut costs.[77]

The public is also poorly informed about the benefit-compounding effects of overlapping programs. Typically, the industry describes welfare income as only the basic cash grant of AFDC, SSI, Social Security, or one of the other cash assistance programs. Yet, as we have seen, a cash grant recipient may be receiving benefits from 15 to 25 other programs which raise his total welfare income to four or five times the value of the cash grant. The public wants the welfare system to provide adequate aid to those who can't work to support themselves, without knowing that, in most cases, adequate or more than adequate aid is already being provided.[78] The industry, on the other hand, wants to increase the numbers of people on welfare, regardless of their ability to support themselves. Every industry-designed reform proposal of the past 15 years has included provisions to allow people with higher assets and incomes to collect welfare benefits.[79]

Welfare programs are funded principally from taxes on earned income, and the public recognizes that the welfare burden can be reduced only if more people work and fewer people need welfare. Thus, the public wants the welfare system to require that those recipients who are able to work get jobs and leave the welfare rolls.[80] The industry response is to seek to add even more people to the rolls by providing welfare to the so-called "working poor"; that is, to those whose earned incomes are less than the multiprogram unearned benefits of the welfare system. In addition, the industry wants to create government jobs for welfare recipients that will enable them to stay on welfare while they work.[81]

Finally, the public apparently believes that there is nothing inherently complicated about providing government welfare to those who need it and withholding it from those who don't, and wants a reformed system that is simple enough to understand. The industry, fearing it will lose control of a system that is simple enough to be comprehensible to the public and Congress, seeks to install more complexity in each new program.[82]

70

Faced with the necessity of reconciling these differences in proposals submitted to Congress, the industry sorts reform ideas into two categories: those that can be manipulated to fit industry goals, and those that can't. Suggestions in the first category are embraced, altered, and perfected by the program change process described earlier. Those in the second category are forcefully opposed.

Nixon, Carter, and the Guaranteed Income

In recent years the welfare industry has sought enactment of a national guaranteed income policy. Although in practice the system provides benefits to anyone "in need," the federal government has never had the authority to set systemwide uniform benefit levels.[83] Assignment of this authority to federal agencies would essentially complete centralization of the welfare system, a major industry goal.[84]

Two concepts have been developed to implement a guaranteed income policy. The first is the concept of family allowances—payments based only on family size and not determined by need. Family allowances were first conceived as a stimulant to population growth by France in 1932, and currently Canada and several European nations have family allowance plans.[85] As a means of implementing a guaranteed income policy, the concept of family allowances is simple and efficient. But as a means of redistributing wealth, the concept is politically unacceptable since it pays the same amounts to rich and poor alike.[86]

The second concept is the negative income tax, originally proposed by economist Milton Friedman in the 1940s.[87] In this concept the government takes taxes from people with incomes above a certain level, just as it does now, but pays "taxes" to people with incomes below that level. As Friedman explained the concept, in 1968:

Under present (1968) law, a family of four (husband, wife, and two dependents) is entitled to personal exemptions and minimum deductions totaling $3,000 ($2,400 personal exemptions, $600 deductions).

If such a family has an income of $3,000, its exemptions and deductions just offset its income. It has a *zero taxable* income and pays no tax.

If it has an income of $4,000, it has a *positive taxable income* of $1,000. Under current law, it is required to *pay* a tax of 15.4 percent, or $154. Hence it ends up with an income after tax of $3,846.

If it has an income of $2,000, it has a *negative taxable income* of –$1,000 ($2,000 minus exemptions and deductions of $3,000 equals –$1,000). This negative taxable income is currently disregarded. Under a negative income tax, the family would be entitled to *receive a fraction* of this sum. If the negative tax rate was 50 percent, it would be entitled to receive $500, leaving it with an income after tax of $2,500.

71

If such a family had no private income, it would have a negative taxable income of -$3,000, which would entitle it to receive $1,500. This is the minimum income guaranteed by this plan for a family of four.

Let me stress the difference between the *break-even income* of $3,000 at which the family neither pays taxes nor receives a subsidy and the *minimum guaranteed income* of $1,500. It is essential to retain a difference between these two in order to preserve an incentive for low-income families to earn additional income.[88]

Friedman envisioned the replacement of all existing welfare programs by the negative income tax.[89] He also proposed transferring the administration of the negative income tax-based welfare system to the Internal Revenue Service, a move calculated to destroy existing federal and state welfare bureaucracies.[90]

In assessing these concepts the industry was faced with a Hobson's choice: a family allowance program would greatly expand industry scope and power but was politically untenable, while a politically appealing negative income tax system would reduce the industry itself to a handful of tax accountants. The dilemma was solved by accepting the negative income tax concept and altering it to conform to industry goals, in a massive application of the industry-controlled program design process. The process has produced a series of conceptually identical reform proposals: the first a guaranteed income proposal prepared for and rejected by the Johnson Administration, the second the Nixon Family Assistance Plan, and the latest the Carter Welfare Reform Plan.[91]

Table 6 summarizes the major steps in the alteration process and relates them to industry goals. Friedman's conception of the negative income tax was in consonance with only one of these goals—system expansion[92]—and partially supported another—centralization—although centralizing welfare administration in the IRS was not acceptable to the industry centered in HEW. The industry's program designers adapted Friedman's concept for the Johnson Administration by restoring administrative control to HEW—thus preserving the welfare bureaucracy—and by limiting application of the negative income tax concept to only two welfare programs—AFDC and SSI—leaving all of the other programs intact and thus salvaging the goals of system complexity and industry employment.

When the Johnson Administration rejected the proposal,[93] the industry added job training and child care provisions—to increase industry employment—and presented it to the Nixon Administration, where it became the Nixon Family Assistance Plan. Although this plan twice failed to pass Congress, the industry has further embellished it with earned income credits—to further expand the welfare population and guarantees of federal jobs for welfare recipients—to further increase industry employment—and it is now being presented as the Carter Welfare Reform Plan.[94]

72

TABLE 6

Conformance of Guaranteed Income Proposals to Industry Goals

Welfare Industry Goals	Friedman's Negative Income Tax Concept	Welfare Industry's Prototype Guaranteed Income Proposal (Rejected by Johnson, 1968)	Nixon's Family Assistance Plan (1969, 1971)	Carter Welfare Reform Plan (1977)
1. Increase welfare population and expenditures.	*Supports industry goal* through guaranteed income for all, which adds "working poor" to existing welfare population.	Incorporates Friedman's concept.	*Supports industry goal* by requiring states to supplement guaranteed income.	*Supports industry goal* by including General Assistance recipients and by raising level of guaranteed income through food-stamp cash out.
2. Centralize welfare system control and administration.	*Partially supports industry goal* by federalizing welfare administration in Internal Revenue Service.	*Fully supports industry goal* by federalizing welfare administration in HEW.	Incorporates prototype proposal, adding Labor to HEW as federal welfare administrators.	Incorporates Nixon's Plan.
3. Increase welfare system complexity.	*Violates industry goal.* Simplifies system by replacing all existing programs with single negative income tax program.	*Supports industry goal* by replacing only two programs with negative income tax, leaving all others intact.	*Supports industry goal* by adding job training and child care service programs.	*Supports industry goal* by adding welfare jobs program.
4. Increase industry employment.	*Violates industry goal.* Reduces industry employment by eliminating federal-state welfare bureaucracies.	*Partially supports industry goal* by restoring bureaucracies to control unreplaced programs.	*Supports industry goal* by increased requirements for welfare workers in new service programs.	*Supports industry goal* by adding government employees through welfare jobs program.

73

Despite the reform rhetoric in which both the Nixon and Carter plans have been bathed, neither is original and neither meets the reform desires of the public. Moreover, both are essentially the same plan, a plan contrived by the welfare industry to make the negative income tax concept fit its goals.

Reform, Reagan Style

In 1971 Ronald Reagan, then governor of California, initiated a welfare reform program that was more closely aligned with public opinion and, consequently, totally at odds with industry goals. Taking the position that government welfare breeds unnecessary and permanent dependency, Reagan set out to reduce or eliminate welfare payments to those with other sources of income, and to make welfare an unattractive alternative to work by requiring able-bodied recipients to perform public service tasks as a condition of getting aid. Savings from these reforms were used to increase aid to the "truly needy," defined as those who were not able to support themselves.[95]

Relying on then-existing state discretionary powers, and using his political strength to obtain waivers of federal regulations, Reagan produced immediate and dramatic results. Within 30 days of the start of the program, California's welfare population of 2.1 million, which had been growing at a rate of 25,000 to 40,000 per month, leveled off and began to drop. In the following two years it declined in actual numbers by 400,000, and in projected numbers by 800,000, while welfare populations in all other large states continued to grow.[96] Welfare expenditure growth slowed from 25 percent to 5 percent a year, even though several hundred thousand "truly needy" recipients received aid increases of up to 30 percent. In the final three years of the Reagan Administration, total welfare expenditures in California were $4 billion under pre-reform estimates.[97] State and county welfare bureaucracies also shrank, and 42 out of the 58 California counties reduced their property tax rates as a result of the Reagan program.

This was not a reform program the industry could bend to its own purposes; it was a direct assault on industry goals. But since it came at the state rather than the federal level, the industry at first underestimated its potential to meet its objectives, and then found that combatting it would require significant changes in federal law—changes that could not be made quickly in the face of Reagan's successes. Stymied, the industry fought holding actions against California—filing court suits to dispute the legalities of the program and imposing bureaucratic delays on state requests for waivers of federal powers—and concentrated its major planning efforts on making sure that the Reagan program would never become a national welfare reform program. In this the industry succeeded. Although several other states have implemented parts of the Reagan program, attempts since 1973 to enact the program through Congress have been easily defeated by industry pressure.[98]

The success of the Reagan program stimulated the industry to push even faster toward its goal of centralizing welfare authority in the federal government, so as to preclude any further attempts by states to reform welfare. The SSI program, designed by the industry and enacted in 1974, virtually eliminated state control of welfare payments to the aged, blind, and disabled; and provisions of the Carter Welfare Reform Plan, carried over from the Nixon Family Assistance Plan, would do the same for family payments.

Welfare Reform Principles

The term "reform" implies a significant departure from past policies and practices. In this sense, the dramatically promoted Carter Welfare Reform Plan, like its conceptual parent, the Nixon Family Assistance Plan, is not a reform at all. Its single innovation—the negative income tax concept—has been altered to extend the policies and accelerate the practices which have in the past increased taxes and dependency and fostered public dissatisfaction. The Carter plan is simply another welfare industry plan, designed to meet industry goals.

On the other hand, the Reagan plan, a true reform, is both undramatic and incomplete. It accomplishes its reforms through technical and unimportant-sounding adjustments to existing programs, and it only affects a handful of programs. Because of this, the industry has been able successfully to characterize it as mere "tinkering" and not real reform.

But both of these plans suffer from a more basic deficiency; they seek reform of the welfare system rather than the welfare industry. It is, after all, the industry which has set the goals for the system and created and administered the programs to meet those goals. To put design of the reform in the hands of the industry—as does the Carter plan—or to attempt to correct the system without reforming the industry—as does the nationally-proposed version of the Reagan plan—is to assure that the future will simply repeat the past.

The first step in welfare reform must be the restructuring and redirection of the welfare industry. Then the welfare system can be revamped to meet public expectations.

Reform of the industry cannot be based on benefit-oriented principles, such as those used to describe the Carter and Reagan plans.[99] The principles for industry reform may be stated most simply as the reverse of the industry's own goals:

1. *Reduce the number of welfare workers.* By encouraging dependency, the welfare system discourages productivity. Thus, the efforts of welfare industry workers actually decrease national productivity. In recent

75

years the growth of welfare industry employment has been due mainly to the expansion of service programs, in which either government employees or government-paid tradesmen provide services to welfare recipients. An effective way to reduce industry employment would be to "cash-out" all service programs, paying the money for the services directly to the recipients and letting them choose and pay for the services they desire. There is ample evidence that welfare recipients, as individuals, spend money at least as wisely as other people;[100] and there is also evidence that organizations paid by the government to serve welfare recipients are often wasteful in expenditure of government funds.[101] The cashing-out of all service programs would put more money and more responsibility for choice in the hands of the welfare recipients, making the extent of welfare benefits clearer to the public. It would also substantially reduce the buying power of the welfare industry, and thus its monopsonistic influence over health care and other welfare-related service trades.

2. *Simplify the welfare system.* The complexity of the welfare system causes most of its unnecessary costs and inequities. Complexity also supports industry control, because no one can understand the system well enough to criticize the system effectively. The cashing-out of all service programs would be the first step to simplification. The next step would be the amalgamation of all welfare programs into one which is based on need and incorporates a financial work incentive. Friedman's original negative income tax is the simplest and most logical concept for such a program,[102] but the design for its implementation must be kept away from the industry. Simplification through a negative income tax program would eliminate the program of overlapping benefits and make welfare administration a relatively inexpensive and routine task.

3. *Decentralize the control of the welfare system.* As long as welfare is centrally controlled within the federal government, the system will be designed and operated to benefit the welfare industry. Decentralization of control and administration, under general guidelines established by Congress, is essential to welfare reform. Decentralization can be accomplished by the transfer of taxing authority for welfare payments to the states, with federal encouragement to the states to further decentralize administration to the local level. This will prevent the industry from rebuilding the existing system through federal and state bureaucracies.

4. *Reduce welfare expenditure growth.* The most important goal of welfare reform must be to reduce expenditure growth, which cannot be sustained at 2.5 to 3 times the growth rate of the national economy. The

steps taken above will remove most of the industry's incentives to create such growth. To make sure these incentives are not restored inadvertently, Congress should closely monitor wealth redistribution in relation to performance of the economy. The amount of wealth redistribution at all levels of government should be explicitly stated and analyzed in the federal budget, and each proposed piece of legislation should include an analysis of its impact on nationwide wealth redistribution.

Welfare reform is a worthy goal, not just politically, but socially and economically as well. The welfare system has failed those who need it and those who pay for it; dependency and taxes have increased in concert. Only the welfare industry has benefitted. And it is the industry which must be reformed if welfare is ever to be refocused on its true purpose: to help those who cannot help themselves.

END NOTES

[1] I have chosen to define welfare as it is normally thought of by the public: government redistribution of wealth to alleviate poverty. As defined here, welfare is totally included in what the Social Security Administration defines as "social welfare," expenditures for which, in 1976, were $331.4 billion (U.S. Social Security Administration, *Social Security Bulletin*, January, 1977). Thus, welfare is slightly more than half of "social welfare."

[2] At the federal level, taxes directly on earned income—personal income and social insurance taxes—made up 75 percent of federal receipts in 1976. Adding that to corporate income taxes which, depending on one's point of view, are either taxes on potential dividends (unearned income) or on potential wages (earned income), taxes on personal income made up 88.5 percent of federal receipts (U.S. Bureau of the Census, *Statistical Abstract of the United States, 1977*, 97th Edition, October, 1976, Table 376). There was a $71.5 billion deficit in 1976, the generally accepted effect of which is to reduce buying power by creating inflation—in essence, another tax on personal income. State and local governments collect 20 percent of their receipts from the federal government and 10 percent from state-imposed income taxes (*Statistical Abstract, 1977*, Table 428). Sales and property taxes make up 45 percent of state and local receipts, but property taxes are predominantly local taxes used to fund non-welfare local services. Probably less than 10 percent of welfare expenditures comes from "wealth" other than personal income, and less than 25 percent from other than earned income.

[3] Data on the number of workers receiving welfare are scarce and inconsistent. In 1974, 62.1 percent of the families below the poverty level earned income from work (U.S. Department of Health, Education, and Welfare, *The Measure of Poverty*, Technical Paper XVIII, Characteristics of Low-Income Populations under Alternative Poverty Definitions, October 1, 1976). Virtually all of these families as well as virtually all individuals below the poverty level receive some form of welfare. In addition, many families and individuals above the poverty level receive some form of welfare. I estimate that at least two-thirds of all welfare recipients either earn income from work or live in families with income from work.

[4] See text, p. 14.

[5] Data on numbers of welfare workers are scarce. This estimate of the number of welfare workers is based on one-half of welfare expenditures used for wages for workers serving welfare recipients, at high average wages of $20,000 a year. See text, pp. 16–17, for estimate of total number of welfare recipients.

[6] The problems, and a few solutions, in calculating the effects of program interactions are enumerated in Joint Economic Committee, Congress of the United States, *Studies of Public Welfare*, Paper No. 1, "Public Income Transfer Programs: The Incidence of Multiple Benefits and the Issues Raised by Their Receipt," December 20, 1973.

[7] Press release: The White House, "Remarks of the President and Joseph A. Califano, Secretary, Department of Health, Education, and Welfare and Dr. F. Ray Marshall, Secretary, Department of Labor, May 2, 1977, 2:00 P.M., p. 1.

[8] The programs are: Public Assistance Payments (AFDC), Supplemental Security Income (SSI), Food Stamps, Work Incentive Program (WIN), and Comprehensive Employment and Training Assistance. Unemployment Insurance and the federal income tax are tangentially affected. The $34 billion estimate for programs included in the reform proposal compares with $187 billion in the entire welfare system in 1976 and more than $220 billion in 1977.

[9] See Daniel P. Moynihan, *The Politics of a Guaranteed Income* (New York: Random House, 1973), pp. 124–134 for description of how the Johnson Administration proposal became the Nixon Family Assistance Plan. See text, pp. 105–110, for analysis of the process which has culminated in the Carter Plan.

[10] System complexity—a major industry goal—both conceals and fosters this phenomenon. See text, pp. 92–93.

[11]See text, pp. 20–24. A reduction in AFDC payments causes off-setting increases in benefits from need-determined programs, including Food Stamps, 5 of the 7 housing programs, General Assistance, Financial Assistance for Higher Education, and Public Assistance Services.

[12]A classic example was reprinted from the Congressional Record, December 3, 1969 in Joint Economic Committee of Congress, *Studies in Public Welfare*, Paper No. 1, p. 35. See also text, pp. 23–24. Reliable calculations of how often this inequity occurs cannot currently be made, because of the complexity of the system and the lack of data about compound benefit levels.

[13]The Carter plan attempts to head off the increased welfare burden on low and middle income families by raising earned income credits on federal tax. This can only work temporarily since, if welfare cost growth continues to outstrip wage growth, tax rates will have to be increased, thus negating the value of the earned income credits.

[14]Principal sources consulted were: U.S. Office of Management and Budget, *Catalog of Federal Domestic Assistance Programs* and *Budget of the United States Government;* U.S. Department of Health, Education, and Welfare, *The Measure of Poverty,* a series of 18 studies published in 1976; the *Social Security Bulletin;* the U.S. Bureau of the Census, *Current Population Reports, State Government Finances* and *County Government Finances;* and Joint Economic Committee of Congress, *Studies in Public Welfare,* 1973.

[15]Sources, in addition to *The Budget of the United States Government,* are: U.S. Bureau of the Census, *State Government Finances* and *County Government Finances;* U.S. Social Security Administration, *Social Security Bulletin;* U.S. Employment and Training Administration, *Unemployment Insurance Statistics;* and U.S. Office of Management and Budget, *Catalog of Federal Domestic Assistance Programs.*

[16]The Work Incentive Program (WIN) is, by law, a joint responsibility of the departments of HEW and Labor.

[17]Examples of programs benefitting all members of a special group, regardless of wealth, are Indian Benefits, Veterans Benefits, Social Security (OASI), and Unemployment Compensation. The Child Nutrition and Elderly Feeding programs, among others, serve all persons in designated "target" areas, regardless of individual financial circumstances.

[18]All years are fiscal years. Statistics in this and following sections summarize data enumerated in the following chapter, "Welfare Programs."

[19]GNP figures are from *U.S. Stat. Abs., 1977* and *1978*, Table 628.

[20]Welfare component only. See program description in the following chapter, "Welfare Programs."

[21]Welfare component only. See program description in the following chapter, "Welfare Programs."

[22]See text, pp. 18–19, and "Financing" sections of program descriptions in the following chapter, "Welfare Programs."

[23]Derived from *The Budget of the United States Government, 1973, 1976,* and *1977; Economic Report of the President,* January 1977; and *U.S. Stat. Abs., 1974* and *1977,* Tables 606 and 708.

[24]Thirty-eight of the 44 programs are managed by these departments. One of the 38—the Work Incentive Program (WIN)—is managed jointly by HEW and Labor.

[25]Percentages do not add to 100 percent because 6 welfare programs are managed by other agencies.

[26]Percentages do not add to 100 percent because 6 welfare programs are managed by other agencies.

[27]Reports in the media of total numbers of welfare recipients are misleading, since they almost invariably refer to only one program, such as AFDC or SSI.

[28]Joint Economic Committee of Congress, *Studies in Public Welfare,* Paper No. 1, pp. iii, 4.

[29]The estimate understates the overlaps among cash assistance programs: Social Security (OASI and DI), Supplemental Security Income (SSI), Public Assistance Grants (AFDC) and Veterans Benefits. Total "beneficiaries" of these programs in 1976 were 52.8 million. SSI

overlaps Social Security by at least 50 percent. AFDC and Veterans Benefits both overlap Social Security and SSI, probably by 25 to 50 percent. The total number of individuals receiving cash payments from these programs probably does not exceed 42 million.

[30]Joint Economic Committee of Congress, *Studies in Public Welfare*, Paper No. 1, pp. 28-29.

[31]E.g. Child Nutrition, Public Health Services, Human Development Services, Community Services, Indian Benefits.

[32]Although Supplemental Security Income (SSI) was enacted in 1974, 2 of its components (Aid to the Aged and Blind) were old programs, enacted in 1935 as parts of the original Social Security Act. The third (Aid to the Totally Disabled) was enacted in 1950.

[33]Workers Compensation and General Assistance were enacted state by state, over an extended period of time starting before the federal programs of the '30s were enacted. Parts of the Indians and Veterans Benefit programs also were enacted before 1930.

[34]Technically, Supplemental Security Income (SSI) was a new law, but in effect it amended the aged, blind, and disabled aid programs by combining them and increasing the degree of federalization.

[35]Unfortunately, as noted previously, there is no way currently to measure its practical extent.

[36]Joint Economic Committee of Congress, *Studies in Public Welfare*, Paper No. 1, p. 35.

[37]All of the food programs except Food Donations; 4 housing programs, 3 which subsidize private rents and 1 which subsidizes college living expenses; all of the health programs; all but 1 (Refugee Assistance) of the cash assistance programs; 5 of the 8 employment and work training programs; both education programs; and all of the service and miscellaneous programs except Indian Benefits.

[38]A possible 2-generation, 17-program package:
Child Nutrition
Food Stamps
Special Supplemental Food (WIC)
Special Milk
Lower Income Housing Assistance
Rent Supplements
Public Health Services
Medicaid
Public Assistance Grants (AFDC)
Work Incentive (WIN)
Employment Service
Financial Assistance for Elementary and Secondary Education
Public Assistance Services (AFDC)
Human Development Services
ACTION Domestic
Legal Services
Community Services
For a possible 3-generation, 24-program package, add:
Elderly Feeding
Medicare (Hospital and Supplemental Medical)
Community Mental Health
Social Security (OASI)
Supplemental Security Income (SSI)
Community Service Employment for Older Americans

[39]Subcommittee on Fiscal Policy, Joint Economic Committee, Congress of the United States, *Income Security for Americans: Recommendations of the Public Welfare Study*, December 5, 1974, pp. 29-49.

[40]The effects of federal welfare programs on charitable contributions for welfare have been drastic. Before 1935, private charities accounted for more than half of welfare expenditures in the United States. In 1975, private contributions for "social welfare" totalled $2.46 billion, or less than 1 percent of the amount spent by the government. American Association of Fund

80

Raising Counsel, Inc., *Giving, USA: 1976 Annual Report*, p. 7 and *Giving in America*, Report of the (Filer) Commission on Private Philanthropy and Public Needs, 1975, pp. 16–17.

[41]Federal welfare managers no longer give even lip service to the goal of reducing dependency. At an HEW management-by-objectives seminar in 1974, the author suggested that, since reducing dependency was supposed to be a primary purpose of the welfare system, the group might pick as an objective reduction of the need for welfare so as to reduce the welfare population. The suggestion was treated as a poor joke, although some of the laughter was nervous.

[42]The "oracle" is Mollie Orshansky; her "need" standards have most recently impacted Supplemental Security Income (SSI), the Nixon Family Assistance Plan, and the Carter Welfare Reform Plan.

[43]"Public assistance introduces problems of race, of sex, of religion, and of family relationships. It is hard to think of four areas most American politicians would rather avoid." Gilbert Y. Steiner, *Social Insecurity: The Politics of Welfare* (Chicago: Rand McNally, 1966), p. 4.

[44]Cash assistance programs have been less susceptible to industry control in two ways. First, state and local governments have had a greater stake, and therefore voice, in cash assistance expenditures, thus diffusing control by the industry's federal headquarters. Second, the industry's relative control over expenditures decreases when money goes directly to welfare recipients, who may not spend it the way the industry wants them to.

[45]In the past 15 years, the welfare industry has purchased increasing percentages of the efforts of physicians, hospitals, pharmacists, medical laboratories, extended care facilities, and domestic attendants. The effects are analyzed in *New Directions in Public Health Care* (San Francisco: Institute for Contemporary Studies, 1976).

[46]Industry decisions are made informally. Agency decisions, when made at all, are made formally, slowly, and in public view. They have little or nothing to do with the way the industry and the welfare system operate and grow. See Thomas E. Borcherding, editor, *Budgets and Bureaucrats: The Sources of Government Growth* (Durham, North Carolina: Duke University Press, 1977).

[47]HEW controls 18 of the 44 welfare programs, and controlled 68 percent of welfare expenditures in 1971 and 63 percent in 1976.

[48]In 1976, $103.1 billion of HEW's $127.7 billion budget was allocated to welfare, as defined here. See U.S. Office of Management and Budget, *The U.S. Budget in Brief, 1977*, p. 64.

[49]Oveta Culp Hobby, 1953–1955
Marion B. Folsom, 1955–1958
Arthur S. Fleming, 1958–1961
Abraham A. Ribicoff, 1961–1962
Anthony J. Celebrezze, 1962–1965
John W. Gardner, 1965–1968
Wilbur J. Cohen, 1968–1969
Robert H. Finch, 1969–1970
Elliot L. Richardson, 1970–1973
Casper W. Weinberger, 1973–1975
F. David Matthews, 1975–1977
Joseph A. Califano, Jr., 1977–

[50]Recent Secretaries who have actively promoted industry-designed programs are Wilbur Cohen (Social Security Act Amendments of 1967), Robert Finch (Nixon Family Assistance Plan). Elliot Richardson (Nixon Family Assistance Plan and Supplemental Security Income), and Joseph Califano (Carter Welfare Reform Plan).

[51]Casper Weinberger has publicly questioned welfare system growth policies, but only since he has left office. Joseph Califano appears to question everything about welfare except industry goals.

[52]The occupants of these positions are mainly Democrats, or at least they have been appointed by Democrats. "In the aftermath of their legislative victories, the Democrats had been able to create a whole new generation of bureaucracies within the government. . ." Moynihan, *Politics of a Guaranteed Income*, pp. 64–65.

[53]See Moynihan, *Politics of a Guaranteed Income*, pp. 124–125.

[54]The process also works in reverse. Several states have hired HEW managers to be state welfare directors. The principal flow, however, is from the states to the federal government. During the 1971 attempt of Ronald Reagan to reform welfare in California, three of the top career administrators in the state welfare department moved to HEW positions.

[55]The most recent threat to the industry—the Reagan California reforms of 1971—brought down upon that state the coordinated wrath of the departments of HEW, Labor, and Agriculture. The most recent opportunity—the Carter Welfare Reform Plan—is a joint product of HEW and Labor.

[56]The U.S. Office of Economic Opportunity (OEO) was the progenitor of both the Community Services Administration and the Legal Services Corporation. OEO's emphasis was on community organization, and quite often it sought confrontations with traditional elements of the industry, such as local housing authorities and welfare departments. A typical industry attitude toward OEO was expressed by former Secretary of HEW Wilbur Cohen in 1971, when he told an audience at the National Bureau of Economic Research that "The OEO program . . . has probably taken three people out of poverty since 1964."

[57]Columbia's Dean is Mitchell I. Ginsberg, former New York Commissioner of Welfare and ardent supporter of the Nixon Family Assistance Plan. Michigan houses Wilbur Cohen, Secretary of HEW under Lyndon Johnson, who was responsible for designing the famous 1967 "30 and 1/3" amendments to the Social Security Act, which allowed workers with substantial earned incomes to retain welfare benefits. Wisconsin designed and conducted, for HEW, the New Jersey negative income tax experiments in the late '60s.

[58]Charles L. Schultze, Edward K. Hamilton, Allen Schick, *Setting National Priorities: The 1971 Budget* (Washington D.C.: The Brookings Institute, 1970), pp. 55–103. Barry M. Blechman, Edward M. Gramlich, Robert W. Hartman, *Setting National Priorities: The 1976 Budget* (Washington D.C.: The Brookings Institute, 1975), pp. 47–84. Henry Owen and Charles L. Schultze, editors, *Setting National Priorities: The Next Ten Years* (Washington D.C.: The Brookings Institute, 1976), pp. 332–345, 505–582.

[59]Mathematica, Inc., performed the statistical analysis for the New Jersey negative income tax experiments in the late 1960s. Mathematica, Inc., and its subsidiary Mathematica Policy Research are authors or co-authors of many current HEW and congressional studies related to welfare assessments and proposals. Among the most recent are: U.S. Department of Health, Education, and Welfare, *The Measure of Poverty*, Technical Paper IX, "Inventory of Federal Data Bases Related to the Measurement of Poverty," Part A; technical support for Congressional Budget Office, *Poverty Status of Families Under Alternative Definitions of Income*, June, 1977; and Mathematica Policy Research, *Analysis of Current Income Maintenance Programs and Budget Allocations, Fiscal Years 1976, 1978, and 1982*, 1977, supported by HEW and the Congressional Research Service.

[60]Principally the UAW and AFL-CIO, which have organized locals among local government employees; the National Association of Social Workers, the "professional" social work organization; the American Medical Association; the American Hospital Association; the National Education Association; the American Federation of Teachers; the National Federation of Federal Employees; and the National Association of Government Employees.

[61]The National Welfare Rights Organization (NWRO) and various state and local organizations of welfare recipients, most of which do not consistently support the NWRO.

[62]The NAACP, the Urban Institute, and the League of Women Voters have all consistently supported industry goals, including the emphasis on services instead of cash assistance.

[63]The National Association of Counties and the National League of Cities have supported federalization of all welfare, on the basis that local governments should not be required to pay for national programs. The National Governors' Conference has vacillated on this issue, most recently supporting federalization.

[64]For example, the NWRO favors cash assistance instead of service programs. Health care providers want program simplification, and the responsibility for payment placed on recipients, to make billing easier. Local unions want administration of welfare to remain the responsibility of local governments, to protect its members.

⁶⁵Recent and notable authors of ideas for change are economist Milton Friedman, Senator Russell Long of Louisiana, and President Carter. All have suffered through the process described here. Friedman saw his negative income tax concept for the replacement of the entire welfare system converted into another program—the Nixon Family Assistance Plan—for welfare expansion (see pp. 106–110). In 1967 Long supported the idea of allowing a welfare mother to deduct $30 plus 1/3 of her earned income for purposes of determining the amount of the welfare grant, a clever subsidy for inexpensive domestic labor in the South. After the idea was enacted, Long saw that its more important effect was to balloon the number of recipients and their income levels in northern cities. In early 1977 Carter promised the nation welfare reform at no additional cost. Six months later, when his industry-altered proposal reached Congress, it called for $2.8 billion in increased welfare spending, and critics said that estimate was far too low.

⁶⁶The most recent example is the 1974 Supplemental Security Income (SSI) program which, though designed primarily by the industry, included some congressionally-imposed provisions to simplify state supplementary payments to the aged and disabled. HEW, ever anxious to complicate the welfare system, ignored the law. In April 1977, the Senate Finance Committee staff issued a detailed report of HEW's transgressions, charging that, among other things, "Departmental policy governing State supplementary benefits departs from clear legislative intent in a way that has distorted the basic purpose of the SSI program . . . the program cannot be permitted to continue to operate in a manner which defies its statutory base" (Committee of Finance, United States Senate, *The Supplemental Security Income Program*, April, 1977, pp. 10–11).

⁶⁷For a detailed explanation and justification of the concept, see Blechman *et. al., Setting National Priorities: The 1976 Budget*, Brookings, pp. 190–207. An official definition and analysis is found in the *The Budget of the United States, Fiscal Year 1976*, pp. 29–32.

⁶⁸*Setting National Priorities: The 1976 Budget*, p. 192.

⁶⁹*Ibid.*, p. 195. The $294.3 billion in "uncontrollable" nondefense expenditures included $149.8 billion (author's estimate) of federal welfare spending.

⁷⁰Congress is reluctant to reduce benefits even when they have been enacted by mistake. It took 5 years (from 1972 to 1977) to remove from law the inadvertent double-counting of inflation in the calculation of social security benefits.

⁷¹CBS News/New York Times Poll on crime, welfare, and job discrimination, *New York Times*, August 3, 1977; Gallup Poll on welfare, *Sacramento Union*, September 9, 1977.

⁷²"Those who take welfare instead of working" are the chronically unemployed on AFDC and the "psychologically" disabled on SSI. "Those who work and also get welfare" are AFDC single-parent families, as well as two-parent families in which the worker works less than 100 hours a month and is therefore technically "unemployed." "Those who get welfare despite the availability of other resources" are social security recipients with large private pensions or investments and those with other sources of income who draw extended unemployment compensation instead of really trying to find work.

⁷³Secretary of HEW Califano estimates that $1 billion, or less than 0.5 percent of total welfare expenditures in 1977, are lost to "fraud, error, and abuse" *(U.S. News and World Report, January 9, 1978, p. 41).

⁷⁴See Note 8 above.

⁷⁵The Nixon Family Assistance Plan covered neither SSI (then aid to the aged, blind, and disabled) nor job training except for the WIN program. It also did not cash-out food stamps.

⁷⁶CBS News/New York Times Poll, *New York Times*, August 3, 1977.

⁷⁷For example, the Reagan welfare reforms in California.

⁷⁸Dividing the 1976 welfare expenditures ($187 billion) by the total number of individual recipients (50 million) produces the startling statistic that in that year the average benefits *per individual* were $3,740. Most welfare expenditures do not go directly to recipients, being spent instead by the government to purchase the services of those who service the recipients. Nevertheless, the value of services by physicians, lawyers, domestic attendants, etc. must be counted as in-kind income to recipients. Thus, the "typical" welfare family of four received, on the average in 1976, cash and in-kind welfare benefits totalling $14,960, an amount slightly

higher than the median family income in that year.

79The most recent is the Carter Welfare Reform Plan, which extends earned income tax credits to families earning as much as $20,000 a year in addition to other welfare benefits (Jane Bryant Quinn, "A Welfare Plan for the Middle Class," *Sacramento* (Calif.) *Bee*, August 17, 1977).

80CBS News/New York Times Poll, *New York Times*, August 3, 1977.

81Quinn, "A Welfare Plan for the Middle Class."

82See text, pp. 92–93.

83A constant complaint of the industry is that welfare payments vary significantly and unfairly from state to state (HEW Secretary Califano in *U.S. News and World Report*, January 9, 1978; Moynihan, *A Guaranteed Income*, pp. 72, 121; Elliot Richardson, *The Creative Balance* (New York: Holt, Rinehart, and Winston, 1976) p. 166. However, the particular programs mentioned— AFDC and, to a lesser extent, General Assistance and Food Stamps—provide only a small fraction of total welfare benefits. When the benefits of all programs are summed, and if geographical variations in cost of living are considered, average benefit levels are probably fairly uniform across the United States.

84Two decentralized programs would remain—Unemployment Compensation and Workers Compensation. The federal government has been slowly encroaching on state control of these programs for several years, and the enactment of a national guaranteed income policy would undoubtedly hasten their complete federalization.

85Moynihan, *A Guaranteed Income*, p. 48.

86Technically, however, family allowances must be considered wealth redistribution, since they constitute a greater percentage of income for a poor family than for a rich one.

87Moynihan (*A Guaranteed Income*, pp. 50–51) has an interesting account of the genesis of the negative income tax concept and its acceptance by "liberals" in the 1960s.

88Milton Friedman, *There's No Such Thing as a Free Lunch* (La Salle, Illinois: Open Court, 1975), pp. 198–199.

89*Ibid.*

90*Ibid.*, p. 203.

91Cf. Moynihan (*A Guaranteed Income*, pp. 124–132) and Richardson (*The Creative Balance*, pp. 167–193). Both are industry supporters; both are writing apologies. Moynihan was closer to the developing situation and, in my opinion, presents a more realistic picture of the bureaucracy in action.

92Friedman believes that implementation of his original concept—the negative income tax as a complete replacement for the existing welfare system—would reduce the incentives to remain on welfare and thus eventually reduce welfare costs and population (Friedman, *There's No Such Thing as a Free Lunch*, pp. 200–201).

93Moynihan, *A Guaranteed Income*, pp. 130–134.

94A concise and readable explanation of the Carter Welfare Reform Plan appeared in *U.S. News and World Report*, August 22, 1977. pp. 42–43.

95For descriptions of the Reagan plan, see Ronald A. Zumbrun *et. al.*, "Welfare Reform: California Meets the Challenge," *Pacific Law Journal*, Vol. 4, No. 2, July, 1973, pp. 739–785; and Charles D. Hobbs, *Ronald Regan's Call to Action* (Nashville-New York: Thomas Nelson, Inc., 1976) pp. 101–103, 173–180.

96Hobbs, *Ronald Reagan's Call to Action*, p. 102.

97*Ibid.*, p. 174.

98Several attempts have been made. The Republican Study Committee in the U.S. House of Representatives produced a proposed National Welfare Reform Act of 1975. In August, 1977, the American Conservative Union announced plans to revive the Reagan concepts as an alternative to the Carter Welfare Reform Plan.

99Press release: The White House, "Remarks of the President and Joseph A. Califano, Secretary, Department of Health, Education, and Welfare and Dr. F. Ray Marshall, Secretary, Department of Labor, May 2, 1977, 2:00 P.M., p. 2. Governor Ronald Reagan, *Meeting the Chal-*

lenge: A Responsible Program for Welfare and Medi-Cal Reform, transmitted to the California Legislature on March 3, 1971.

[100]For example, "The Poor Use Cash Wisely, Study Shows," *Sacramento Bee,* September 21, 1977

[101]For example, "Poverty Program Groups Toss Cash Around?" *Sacramento Bee,* October 21, 1977.

[102]This is difficult to explain, as Moynihan points out (*A Guaranteed Income,* p. 139).